MW01124502

YOUR ROAD TO *Yes!*

HOW TO BUILD TRUST IN YOURSELF AND WITH OTHERS

MAY YOUR PRESENCE MAKE THE
WORLD A KINDER, GENTLER, AND
MORE TRUSTING PLACE.

YOUR ROAD TO YES!
by Justin Patton

Printed in the United States of America.
FIRST EDITION, June 2022.

ISBN 978-1-7328766-9-9 (paperback)
ISBN 978-1-7328766-8-2 (ebook)

Cover design and layout by Shaina Nielson

Mom,

Being your kid is the greatest gift of our lifetime.

You've taught us the importance of family. You remodeled resiliency more times than what might have felt fair. You reminded us to laugh and not take ourselves or others too seriously. You weren't afraid to challenge us, but you had our back in the process. You always made us feel welcome, loved, and wanted.

Thank you for being a demonstration that trust isn't about always getting it right, but it's about the commitment to always figure it out together.

Your life and your presence have changed us for the better.

We love you...

JUSTIN PATTON

PRAISE FOR
YOUR ROAD TO *Yes!*

"Justin reminds us that the key to building a thriving workplace culture is creating a space where people feel they belong. That only happens through trust. *Your Road to Yes!* should be on every leader's bookshelf."
Greg Creed, Retired CEO at Yum! Brands

"Justin has thoughtfully constructed *Your Road to Yes!* to be both provocative and applicable. His insights encourage you to challenge yourself, and his approach equips you with your own roadmap to building trust in yourself and with others. I would recommend this book to anyone who wants to make the lives of others consistently better, or simply wants to go forward, better."
Kelly McCulloch, Global Chief People Officer at Taco Bell

"When it comes to building trust, some of the world's most prominent organizations rely on Justin Patton for expert advice. In particular, he's especially gifted in helping them build trust in environments that are competitive and fast-moving. If trust is a priority in your organization, Patton's *Your Road to Yes!* is an important read."
Mark Levy, Differentiation expert at Levy Innovation LLC

"Justin's book goes in-depth on what it takes to build trust with others: transparency, tact, and togetherness. The humor, relatable stories, and actionable insights are what make *Your Road to Yes!* an important read for anyone who believes relationships are the key to success."
Suzanne Bohle, Executive VP at Council of State Restaurant Associations

"Justin reminds us that connection and authenticity are a result of trust, and trust is our biggest competitive advantage. His book moves from just talking about trust to demonstrating how you bring those concepts to life personally and professionally."
Tony Buford, Division VP at KBP Brands

"Trust is a word that is overused and an action that is underexplored. Justin invites us to change that with this book, exploring it in ourselves and with others. I'm now a better at recognizing it, and more importantly, at building it."
Nicholas Bertram, President at The GIANT Co.

"*Your Road to Yes!* is a must-read book for every leader. It will challenge you to look differently at how you show up, communicate, and bring out the best in others."
George Dockins, Executive Director at Public School Employees of Washington

2

"Justin has a unique gift. He can take the most delicate of human insights and with humor, help us accept our humanity. Then he challenges us to take one more step on our path towards being greater expressions of our beautiful selves. Justin's book on trust is a gift of insights and actions."
Monica Rothgery, Chief Operations Officer at KFC

"Justin has shared essential tools for growing as a leader and reminds us that trust is a foundational element in the relationship we have with ourselves and with our team. It is the key to loyalty, engagement, and opportunity. Your Road to Yes! challenges every person to rethink how they show up for themselves and for others."
Terri Steeb Gronau, NCAA VP of Division II

"Relationships are not easy. Every day is a lesson on trust. The most meaningful relationships in our lives have trust as their foundation. Our actions determine our trustworthiness, and our power lies in our choices. *Your Road to Yes!* is a must-read book for every leader and will challenge you to look differently at how you show up, communicate, and bring out the best in others."
Sheila Arquette, President & CEO at National Association of Specialty Pharmacy

"This book provides great insight into the behaviors that build and destroy trust in ourselves, others, and our businesses. You have probably heard that trust is earned— well, in this book Justin outlines clearly how to build and sustain it to achieve breakthrough results while strengthening relationships along the journey. This book is a must-read for those either aspiring to influence others or accountable for an entire business."
Dave Hare, Director of Enterprise Learning and Development at GE Appliances

"*Your Road to Yes!* brings together the concepts I've seen Justin apply with many leaders in our company. Justin has worked with our leadership teams in both group settings and, for the past year and a half, as a one-on-one executive coach for several of our multi-unit leaders. I am a witness to how his message on trust works."
Scott Shepherd, Chief Operating Officer at Pacific Bells, Inc.

"Real trust is never a by-product of transactions. It's based on experiences deeming a relationship worthy of trust. Justin Patton gets it and explains well the nature and importance of trust for any leader or organization."
Captain Dave Tuck, Pilot with United Airlines

"*Your Road to Yes!* will challenge you on how you view communication and connection. Read it, do the work, and feel the difference that greater trust brings to every interaction."
Vicki Halsey, VP Applied Learning at Ken Blanchard Companies

CONTENT

01 Every Day is a Lesson on Trust — 06

02 Trust is Your Biggest Competitive Advantage — 18

03 Silence is Your Biggest Threat — 30

04 Building Trust in Yourself — 40

05 Building Trust with Others

68

06 Factors that Erode Trust

112

07 How to Repair Trust
Once It's Broken

130

08 Now It's Up To You

152

JUSTIN PATTON

CHAPTER ONE

EVERY DAY IS A LESSON ON TRUST

*Trust is the belief
You will always have my back
And I will have yours.*

YOUR ROAD TO YES!

Every day is a lesson on trust. When you get out of bed, you trust that your water and electricity will work if you pay the bills on time. You trust your family will do right by you. You trust other drivers on the road to stay in their lane and not cross that double yellow line. You trust that the restaurant food you eat is safe. You trust that Lindsay Lohan will make a Hollywood comeback. Okay, so maybe that last one was my wishful thinking, but the point is that trust is an integral part of our life every day. The most meaningful relationships in our lives are a result of trust. This feeling of trust between you and the other person allows you to show up authentically, openly share your perspective, forgive, and stay more engaged.

My earliest memory of trust happened when I was around seven years old. My friend had called and told me to meet him down the street. I threw the door open, ran outside barefoot, jumped on my bike, and started peddling. At some point, I put my head back and lifted my feet. As I tried to recenter myself on the bike, my right big toe got caught in the spoke of my bicycle wheel. My bike came to an immediate halt, I went flying over the handlebars, and blood poured onto the hot pavement.

Someone must have run to my house and got my dad because the next thing I saw was him running down the street. My dad was an Air Force veteran and a tough guy who didn't show much emotion. I expected him to say, "Suck it up, son! You're fine." However, this time was different. He didn't do that. Instead, he picked me up and carried me back to the house. He sat me on the edge of the kitchen sink and started to **TRUST IS THE UNWAVERING BELIEF THAT YOU WILL HAVE MY BACK.**

doctor up my toe. Of course, I was screaming like the toe had fallen off. Looking back, my dad treated me so gently at that moment, which is why this is my earliest memory of trust. He taught me…

Trust is the unwavering belief that you will have my back.

Every action you take and every choice you make signals to others whether you have their back. Think about that for a moment! How you act in a difficult conversation, express yourself when you're exhausted, communicate with people at work, and respond when people need you the most teach others whether they should continue to trust you or not.

Millions of people will wake up today and feel their boss or colleagues do not have their back. The organization will then wonder why their people aren't as engaged as they'd like and why the vision for the culture only lives on the walls in people's offices – not in the day-to-day interactions between people.

TRUST IS ALWAYS THE RESULT OF EFFECTIVE COMMUNICATION.

You deserve relationships, whether at work or home, where trust and belonging are the foundation. That requires everyone involved to take responsibility for how they communicate. Trust is always the result of effective communication. The words, body language, and intensity we consistently display influence whether people believe we have their back. I've designed this book to challenge the way you think about trust but, more importantly, give you specific actions to help you create an environment where trust is present.

RESEARCH ON THE IMPACT OF TRUST

It's important to talk about why trust matters before we jump right in and talk about how to build it in ourselves and with others. Our mindset around trust shapes how we cultivate it, the expectations we hold others to, and the value we place on it in our lives. I think there is general agreement among most of us that trust is important, but I'm not convinced that everyone knows its tangible outcomes in business. Sometimes, often unconsciously, we prioritize our smarts, independence, or work ethic over the ability to be trustworthy. Those things are valuable and important and will impress and wow people in the short term, but trust is how you win the long game. And I always want you to play the long game. Let's take a moment to discuss why trust is vital to every workplace.

The Society for Human Resource Management (SHRM) conducted a survey in 2020, and the results reinforced the adage, "People don't leave <u>companies; they leave managers</u>." In fact, 84 percent of respondents said poorly trained managers create a lot of unnecessary work and stress. The top skill responders said managers could improve on was communicating effectively. That's significant. Managers must learn to communicate in ways that build trust versus focusing on transactions. "Soft skills" hold managers back, not a lack of knowledge.

SHRM's research findings are congruent with Gallup, who previously cited that 50 percent of employees leave their companies because of their boss. In 2021, Gallup also noted, "For the first year in more than a decade, the percentage of engaged workers in the U.S. declined in 2021. Just over one-third of employees (34 percent) were engaged." This is significant, and we should all care. The way employees show up in their job will impact the experience customers receive.

Greg Creed, former CEO of Yum! Brands and Taco Bell, used to say, "The customer's experience will never exceed the team member's experience." We all communicate on the level of our energy. If we're happy, engaged, and enjoy the people we work with, then the customers are going to benefit from that experience. If we're only showing up because we need a paycheck and we don't really like the manager or people we work with, customers will get a second-rate experience.

Pew Research Center studied trust-related issues in America in 2019 and issued their findings in a report called "Trust and Distrust in America." Seventy-one percent of adults believe Americans are less confident in each other than they were twenty years ago. Contributing factors to that statistic include isolation and loneliness, polarization in government, social media, and bias in news media. One man was cited as saying, "Everything is more polarized, and it is generally more difficult to disagree with someone, come to a general understanding, and move on."

The Workforce Institute at UKG surveyed nearly four thousand employees and business leaders in eleven countries on the state of trust in June 2020. In their research document, "Trust in the Modern

Workplace," they report, "<u>Only 18 percent of employees have told their manager they were interviewing for another job in order to receive their guidance and opinion.</u>" That finding would indicate that employees do not feel the relationship can handle the truth or that it's not worth bringing it up and dealing with the potential fallout. The employee has already decided to go at things on their own versus including their manager in the process. This is a clear indication of a lack of trust in the relationship. I believe this mindset of trust is dangerous and only reinforces the divide in trust between managers and employees.

All the research highlights that trust is waning, impacting every corner of our lives. The COVID pandemic hasn't made the building of trust any easier. "The Great Resignation" is a term coined by Anthony Klotz, a professor of management at Texas A&M University. Others have altered the phrase: "The Great Reevaluation," "The Great Escape," and "The Great Upgrade" are all popular nomenclatures. This term describes the mass exodus of people from the labor market during the COVID pandemic. The pandemic opened people's eyes to their environments and whether those environments were serving them. Regardless of what we call it, people are reevaluating themselves, what they're willing and unwilling to put up with, and what they want in their lives.

People want a sense of security in a world that feels in turmoil. They want to be in environments that challenge them to use their skills but are also fun, flexible, and create fellowship. They want transparent, authentic relationships that make them feel less alone. We must get back to genuine relationship building, and trust is how we do it.

IS TRUST GIVEN, OR IS IT EARNED?

When I first started my research on trust, I'd often ask people, "Do you think trust is given or earned?" The answers always varied and usually had a lot to do with one's past experiences. The Workforce Institute at UKG's research, documented in "Trust in the Modern Workplace: Why is Trust Still Hard to Find at Work?" found that "Sixty-eight percent of US employees and business leaders say trust must be earned." The problem with this mindset is that everyone is waiting around for everyone else to earn their trust while no one is giving it. Trust can't flourish in an environment where everyone waits for someone else to begin.

(I believe trust is built. The mutual giving and earning of trust builds healthy relationships and workplaces.)

Our ability to give trust to others happens from our heart space. It's vulnerable and can feel risky because there's no guarantee of what people will do with the trust we give them. Think of giving trust as tandem skydiving. You must be willing to jump into the adventure with someone, let go of control, and trust that the other person will do their part to make the journey successful. It can feel scary. Giving trust looks like opening up and sharing your feelings or ideas with someone. It's a manager putting someone on a high-profile project because they believe they are ready. It's also a kid coming to their parent and letting them know they messed up. It takes courage to give trust to others. That only comes from our heart space.

It is equally as important that we watch what people do with the trust we give them — that we step back and think objectively about their actions. Their impact on trust in the relationship will determine whether they earn more trust from us. The earning of trust happens from our head space. We watch to see if people follow through on their commitments. We notice if they keep what we shared with them confidential, and we observe if they take accountability when things don't go as planned.

If you try to build trust from only your head space, you are typically reluctant, hold everyone at arm's length, and keep a scorecard where everyone must prove themselves worthy. That's emotionally exhausting for the other person. If you try to build trust from only your heart space, you typically allow your emotions to cloud any rational decision-making, ignore warning signs, and justify bad behavior. That's emotionally exhausting for you. Building trust takes effort, but it shouldn't be emotionally exhausting.

BUILDING TRUST TAKES EFFORT, BUT IT SHOULDN'T BE EMOTIONALLY EXHAUSTING.

Building trust is a delicate balancing of both head and heart, but it always starts with heart. The best leaders I've known and studied all had the self-trust and willingness to extend a base level of trust to others, but they paid attention. They watched what people did with the trust they extended, and that information told them how to show up in the relationship moving forward.

Colin Powell highlights this lesson in his book *It Worked for Me: In Life and Leadership*. He said, "I believe that when you first take over a new outfit, start out trusting the people there unless you have real evidence not to. If you trust them, they will trust you, and those bonds will strengthen over time. They will work hard to make sure you do well. They will protect you and cover you. They will take care of you."

TRUST IS ON THE LINE IN EVERY CUSTOMER INTERACTION.

Customers give us a base level of trust when they buy one of our products. They believe our product will add value to their lives. They also believe our product will perform as described. They purchase with their heart space and watch what happens from their head space. If the product and company live up to the customer's expectations, they earn a little more trust. That's how you gain loyal customers. If the product doesn't live up to their expectations, one of two things happens. They take their trust somewhere else and invest in someone new or raise their concerns and give us a chance to do right by our relationship with them. Either way, trust is on the line in every customer interaction.

Trust is also on the line every day in the workplace. Let me be frank: Management sucks sometimes, but I also believe management changes lives and influences a company's overall success. Managers building trust with their teams (and vice versa) should be of utmost priority in every organization.

Employees give their managers a base level of trust when they accept a job. They trust their manager will have their back, give them the tools to do their job effectively, and regularly communicate, so they are never blindsided. Managers earn that trust daily when they check in, recognize efforts, provide the feedback employees need to grow, keep sensitive information confidential, and make their team members part of the decision-making process.

Managers also give employees trust the moment they decide to hire them. They trust that you will deliver on what you said you could do in the interview. They understand that you will not know how to do everything, but they trust that you'll listen, be open to feedback, and make the appropriate changes to set up the team and company for success. Employees earn trust with their managers when they deliver on the results promised, communicate effectively, and demonstrate that they're team players.

The constant giving and earning of trust builds high levels of trust in any relationship. Relationship expert John Gottman states, "Trust is built in very small moments." He explains that every moment gives us a choice to build trust with the other person or turn away and lose trust. This incremental giving and earning of trust between two people allow connection and loyalty to happen.

It's the deliberate giving and earning of trust in a relationship that allows trust to be built. You cannot be selfish and expect to have high levels of trust with others. Rather, trust requires you to put the relationship before your ego. Trust is not built in the wishing for, praying for, hoping for, or thinking about. Trust is built in the doing.

TRUST IS BUILT IN THE DOING.

TRUSTING RELATIONSHIPS ARE BUILT ON YES

Think about a relationship where you have high levels of trust. Who comes to mind for you? I think about my mom. Carol Chapman is the most resilient woman I know. She almost died from being born three months premature. She overcame relationships where people didn't treat her the way she deserved, and she managed to pull herself back up after losing my father long before she ever should have. Her ability to rise up, again and again, has earned my admiration, but it's how she has shown up for me for the past forty-two years that built the trust between us. I've always felt I could talk with my mom if I needed support, advice, or to get something off my chest. She was always there for the relationship. But I want to be clear on something: that doesn't mean the relationship has always been perfect or comfortable. Relationships with high levels of trust aren't a result of everything being comfortable all the time. Trust is sometimes uncomfortable. There have been moments where Mom and I disappointed each other, didn't live up to each other's expectations, and had to engage in uncomfortable conversations that involved some tears. But we always got through it, and the vulnerability and intimacy we shared only built stronger trust. My mom has taught me that you can love a person while showing them grace as they navigate their way through life. Mom and I never gave up on each other, and we always loved our relationship enough to figure the journey out together. Regardless of what we went through, we were always able to say "YES!" to the three questions below:

> - Do they take me with them along the journey?
> - Do they create a safe space for me to open up?
> - Do they make me feel less alone in the world?

Our ability to say "YES!" to these three questions is what all high-trust relationships have in common. It reassures us that we have each other's backs. My hope for you is that you're in relationships where you can answer, "Yes!"

If trust is low in our relationships, it's often because we cannot say "YES!" to one or more of these questions. However, it's often easy to identify how others are not showing up in our relationships because it prevents us from doing the necessary, challenging work of looking at ourselves and owning our part in the breakdown. We can't control how others show up, but we have complete control and responsibility for our own energy. Therefore, this book empowers you to <u>focus on what you can do to build trust</u>. Instead of asking the questions in the third person, we are going to ask the questions in the first person:

YOUR ROAD TO YES!

A
B
C

- Do I take people with me along the journey?
- Do I create a safe space for people to open up?
- Do I make people feel less alone in the world?

You build high levels of trust in a relationship when you can answer yes to all three of these foundational questions. These questions are not random but rather tie back to the three core factors of building trust with others, which we dive into later in the book. Those core factors are transparency, tact, and togetherness.

Sometimes you might answer yes to only one or two of those questions. There lies the opportunity for improvement. Relationships are not easy. Two people drag in their baggage and try to figure out how to make it work together. Some moments are amazing, and other moments are confusing. Regardless, you deserve to be with someone who communicates transparently, cares about your feelings, and wants to spend time with you.

Trust is a feeling verified by actions. People care more about what you do than what you say. Your actions determine your trustworthiness. It's not just one significant action or one good day that makes someone trustworthy (Over time, our collective and repetitive choices build trust incrementally, proving that the small things really do matter.)

TRUST IS A FEELING VERIFIED BY ACTIONS.

My best friends are my best friends because they are there for me when I need them. They check in with me for no other reason than to see how I'm doing. They're vulnerable and share intimate truths about their hopes and fears with me. They love me enough to hold me accountable in a gentle way. They listen without judgment, follow through on their commitments, own up to their mistakes, and celebrate my wins. I do the same for them. This deep level of trust we've built has happened through one small choice after another. I believe these choices are just as important personally as they are professionally. This is how leaders earn the trust of their followers over time. Trust in every relationship is built one yes at a time, and the goal for all of us is to be in relationships built on yes.

TRUST DOESN'T GET AN OFF DAY

I opened the book by saying that every day is a lesson on trust. Those lessons either bring you closer to the types of relationships you want or further away. Trust doesn't get an off day, so leaders must take responsibility for the energy they show up with every day and in every moment. That doesn't mean we're always going to get it right, but we try. With that trying comes intentionality, and as a result, we get it right way more often than we get it wrong. That makes a big difference!

The road to yes isn't easy. It takes time and the consistent giving and earning of trust. Some people might think that sounds exhausting, but I find it liberating. I believe we feel lighter when we can be in relationships where we don't have to play a part, can openly communicate, and know that someone isn't walking out in the challenging moments. What's more exhausting is feeling like you must dance around someone's temper, withhold how you really feel, not express what you need, and feel as though you have the responsibilities of a relationship but are still alone.

TRUST IS THE DRIVING FACTOR IN OUR ABILITY TO LEAD, LOVE, AND COMMUNICATE EFFECTIVELY IN EVERY RELATIONSHIP.

Our ability to say "YES!" in our relationships influences how we show up in them and whether we feel connected. You deserve to be in a space of trust and belonging, whether at home or work. Trust is the driving factor in our ability to lead, love, and communicate effectively in every relationship. I believe that's what we all ultimately want, whether we know how to make that happen or not. We must create habits that get us to yes, and this book is your guide on how to make that happen. Your choices should always lead to yes!

CHAPTER ONE
SUMMARY

- Every day is a lesson on trust.

- Trust is the unwavering belief that you will have my back.

- Trust is always the result of effective communication.

- Building trust takes effort, but it shouldn't be emotionally exhausting.

- Trust is on the line in every customer interaction.

- Trust is built in the doing.

- Trust happens when both people can answer yes to three foundational questions: Do I take people with me along the journey? Do I create a safe space for people to open up? Do I make people feel less alone in the world?

- The goal for all of us is to be in relationships built on yes.

- Trust is a feeling verified by actions.

- Trust doesn't get an off day.

- Trust is the driving factor in our ability to lead, love, and communicate effectively in every relationship.

- Your choices should always lead to "Yes!"

CHAPTER TWO

TRUST IS YOUR BIGGEST COMPETITIVE ADVANTAGE

*Trust is your biggest
Competitive advantage.
It brings people back.*

YOUR ROAD TO YES!

At sixteen, I started my first job working the drive-thru and front counter at McDonald's. I thought I had made it, y'all. I loved going to work every day, connecting with customers, and earning my own money. It didn't hurt that I got free food on my lunch break. I would often take my time cleaning the lobby because it allowed me the opportunity to connect with guests. In the drive-thru, I was keenly aware that we had the chance to be the best part of someone's day. I acknowledged people, loved when they had their pets, and tried to make them feel seen. In my desire to connect with customers, I had a manager who often told me I needed to speed things up. It was the first time I heard the classic line: "Time is money!"

Now, is there some truth that time equals money? Sure. We want to respect people's time. We want processes to be efficient. We understand that the more cars you get through a drive-thru, the more money you make. But who cares if you meet your time metric if the experience wasn't memorable? I was a closing keynote speaker at the AKFCF (Association of Kentucky Fried Chicken Franchisees) convention in 2022 when I heard Monica Rothgery, the company's Chief Operations Officer, say, "It's better to be slower and make it right than be fast and wrong." YES! YES! It's the connection, not the transaction we create during the experience, that allows us to slowly start to build trust and, in time, repeat customers.

We live in a society where we often glorify busyness, and we're rushing everywhere we go. As a result, we rush others. We need to stop. It's not serving our relationships. We have become so accustomed to rushing into meetings and out the door with our kids that we miss pivotal moments to build deeper levels of trust.

We all lose when we prioritize time over trust. Therefore, the more important conversation we should have is how *trust is money*. Let me prove it. Have you ever stopped purchasing someone's services or products because of one negative experience? Many of us have. And time is generally not the contributing factor to why we never went back. We stop doing business with companies that break our trust.

WE ALL LOSE WHEN WE PRIORITIZE TIME OVER TRUST.

Years ago, I was standing in line at a popular Mexican restaurant where they make your food right in front of you. I ordered a chicken quesadilla and asked for it to be grilled twice. I waited patiently for the timer to go off. After the second time, the young lady making my food hit the button for the third time. I politely leaned forward and said, "Excuse me, ma'am. I only wanted it cooked twice." She cranked her head around slowly like Linda Blair from *The Exorcist*, looked straight at me, lifted her eyebrows, and said, "I KNOW!" She plopped my quesadilla on the counter, slid it slowly towards me, and walked off as if on an episode of *America's Next Top Model*. Her presence was so dismissive that I immediately tweeted their corporate headquarters, told everyone I could about the experience, and never returned.

THE BEST BUSINESSES WILL ALWAYS FIND A WAY TO EXCEL IN BALANCING BOTH TIME AND TRUST.

My negative experience at this restaurant had nothing to do with time. Instead, they sacrificed my trust in their desire to meet their time commitments. This worker was unaware, or didn't care, about the impact her presence had on me and others. Organizations who sacrifice trust to meet time constraints are doing themselves and their customers a disservice. The best businesses will always find a way to excel in balancing both time and trust.

This experience taught me that trust is your biggest competitive advantage because it leads to more teamwork, candor, loyalty, and opportunity. Make trust a business priority and watch what loyalty does to your finances. The best leaders use their presence to earn and keep others' trust, and the best organizations use their products and services to earn and keep the trust of their customers.

TRUST LEADS TO TEAMWORK

Trust naturally leads to better teamwork because you commit to prioritizing the relationship. Your goal is to make the other person feel like they're part of a team, so keep your ego in check, spend time together, and include each other in decisions.

Trust always leads to teamwork because you believe that other people's contributions make you better and more successful. Yes, you could probably make it by yourself, but trust is knowing you don't have to. You see things differently when you choose to believe that. You acknowledge people for what they bring to the relationship instead of focusing on everything you wish they'd do differently. You appreciate the gifts and talents they demonstrate that you do not possess. You recognize that you can get further, faster if you work together.

I interviewed some NCAA athletes on trust and its role on their team. They taught me that "The game does not build trust. It tests it." They explained that everything happens so quickly during competition that you instinctively default to what you know. If a culture of mistrust is created outside the field, it will be carried onto the field when it matters. If the team believes in each other, spends quality time together, and values each person's strengths, that is what gets carried onto the field. Do not expect to have trust in the high-pressure moments if you haven't taken the time to build it before then. This concept applies just as much in business as in a sports competition. You never build trust in the middle of the game; the game is where you find out how much trust you've built. Trust is the key to competing at your best by making better team players.

> **THE GAME DOES NOT BUILD TRUST. IT TESTS IT.**

TRUST LEADS TO CANDOR

Candor is your ability to be both open and honest with your expression. Trust—both in yourself and with others—opens the door for more authentic candor. Without it, we make assumptions about what things mean. We hold back and don't say the things we need to say. We ultimately get resentful and start to check out of relationships.

The quality of our relationships can be measured by the level of candor in them. When you can engage in candid conversations as friends, team, couple, or family, you role-model that this is a space where people can discuss important, hard, vulnerable things. When there's a lack of candor in a relationship, there's a lack of trust either in oneself, the other person, or both.

While running Anthem's national sales training department, I set up a peer mentor group for some new leaders. These leaders met once a week for three months. During their meetings, they each shared something they needed help with or support on. The structure of this group encouraged candor. These leaders built trust due to their willingness to hear and support each other over the months. In fact, the program went so well that the leaders continued meeting even after the program officially ended.

(Alcoholics Anonymous, church Bible study, and group therapy create spaces for people to feel less alone in the world, share their thoughts and feelings, and explore new ways of showing up. These spaces have created a structure for trust and candor to flourish. As a result, the people in these groups feel highly connected. When we feel connected, we feel safe enough to keep opening up.)

My best friend and I recently had a deep conversation on mental health. She shared that someone she knows tried to commit suicide. We talked about the loneliness and pain that so many people feel. We talked about times in our lives when we felt that pain. This exchange led to a conversation around how sports teams, fraternities and sororities, and other familial groups have a unique opportunity to bring together their members and create an environment where each person answers the following question: "What are you currently struggling with?"

Some people might answer that they're struggling to balance work and sports. Some might share that they're in a relationship that isn't going well and don't know what to do. Others might say they're just struggling to decide on a particular topic. It doesn't matter how they respond. What matters is that we create the space for emotional expression.

Most people don't bear their soul in just one conversation. They test the waters, watch how others jump in, and evaluate people's reactions. The safer they feel, the more deeply into the water they wade. Leaders have a responsibility to encourage hard but safe conversations. You are that leader. When combined with safety, candor gives people the space to share what lurks under the surface that they've been too afraid to acknowledge. It's then that we build more trust with each other and more trust with ourselves.

TRUST LEADS TO LOYALTY

Stephen R. Covey, in his bestselling book *The 7 Habits of Highly Effective People*, emphasizes that all relationships establish an "emotional bank account." This account is not made up of money but trust between you and the other person. You have one with your kids, family members, coworkers, boss, and customers. We must continuously invest in those emotional bank accounts because there will come a point in any long-term relationship where you mess up, have a bad day, or don't act from your highest self. In those moments, you make a withdrawal of trust. It's then that you get to see if there are enough emotional deposits in the account to survive what happened. All relationships end when people become emotionally bankrupt. This occurs when one person takes more out of the emotional bank account than they invested. Eventually, the other person in the relationship will stop putting up with someone's overdrafts and walk away. Every action you take or don't take is an investment or a withdrawal of trust. The more deposits we make, the more trust grows. The more trust grows, the longer we stay in the relationship. Trust always leads to more loyalty and engagement.

> ALL RELATIONSHIPS END WHEN PEOPLE BECOME EMOTIONALLY BANKRUPT.

There is research to back this up. Paul J. Zak, author of *The Neuroscience of Trust*, highlights that "Respondents whose companies were in the top quartile [of trust] indicated they were 76 percent more engaged at work…50 percent planned to stay with their employer over the next year, and 88 percent said they would recommend their company to family and friends as a place to work."

Think of a brand you are loyal to as a customer. What transpired over time for them to earn that level of loyalty from you? For me, that is Delta Airlines. There are a lot of airlines to fly, and I've flown most of them. But my experience on Delta has always been better. The price of tickets is comparable to other airlines, and the seats are more comfortable. As I invested in the relationship, they invested back in me with frequent flyer miles and resulting status upgrades. The relationship became a win-win for both of us. I give them my business, and they give me a consistent experience I can rely on each time. I have a dedicated number to call when I have an issue. I typically get upgraded on my flights. And they are flexible when I need to make changes. Don't get me wrong. Not every experience has been excellent. We've had our share of relationship squabbles, but we've had more good moments than bad. We've put more trust deposits into each other's accounts than we've taken out. As a result, that trust has created a sense of loyalty that continues today.

TRUST LEADS TO OPPORTUNITY

We live in a world where we constantly crash in and out of people's lives. The reality is that most people will never know us at the level of our family and close friends. Most people in this life will only catch glimpses of who we are. They will make judgments about us based on those glimpses, and those judgments will impact which doors open and which ones close. We must manage the glimpses that people see, which requires us to take responsibility for the energy we show up with every day. That level of consistency creates trust, and trust always leads to more opportunities in life.

In 2012, a Taco Bell leader asked me to co-facilitate the largest leadership development program in the company's history for restaurant general managers. The program was called theMARK, a three-day experience that challenged leaders to think about the mark they leave in every area of their life. It was a soul-searching journey around their values, purpose, how they show up or don't show up to the people they say are important, and what they feel they need to do differently to be better leaders in all areas of their lives. The program was so successful that it created a partnership for over a decade. The trust we built together over the years has ignited more opportunities. It has allowed me to speak in front of franchisee groups, coach executives in the restaurant support center, join the top general managers at their annual award celebration in Hawaii, work with other restaurant companies, and more.

Think back on your last job interview. How did it go? What do you think the hiring manager and/or committee looked for? Yes, they want someone with technical knowledge who they believe can do the job. That's why they spend time looking at your resume and asking you questions. However, they're also looking for someone they believe others would want to work with daily. They're looking for someone they think would fit in with the team and hopefully bring an insightful, much-needed perspective. By the final round of interviews, I believe they usually hire someone based on feeling. They hire the person they trust will be able to bring the best into the organization. Your ability to create trust in a short amount of time created that opportunity for you or someone else.

I believe three specific actions make someone an invaluable asset to their manager and an organization: their consistent ability to get results, make their manager's life easier, and be a team player. These actions cultivate trust, which is why the people who perform them tend to get designated as "high performers." They become the go-to person for their manager, and opportunities and additional exposure flow their way. If that boss ever leaves the company, they will typically try to recruit these individuals to work with them at the new organization when the time is right. Again, trust leads to opportunity and is an abundance generator in your life.

Finally, think about the last recommendation you received from someone you trust. Maybe it was about where to eat, a vacation destination, or a book to read. Regardless, you tend to rank that recommendation higher than a recommendation from someone you don't know. If you decide to act on the information you received, then that information, and the person who dispensed it, generated opportunity for that restaurant, vacation spot, or author. That opportunity would likely not have come had someone who trusted their services not recommended it. Trust creates opportunity and a consistent source of revenue.

TRUST IS YOUR BIGGEST COMPETITIVE ADVANTAGE

Teamwork, candor, loyalty, and opportunity are all elements that help produce great workplace culture. They are all a result of trust. The way leaders show up and communicate every day in the workplace ultimately decides the organization's culture. Your organization's culture should be adding strategic value to the overall business. The culture should motivate employees to want to stay and provide customers with a better experience. It should also facilitate the development of a diverse talent pipeline that sets up the company for future success. If it's not, you're not as competitive as you need or could be, and you will lose people to workplaces that promise and deliver on an environment of trust and belonging.

Trust is your biggest competitive advantage because it keeps people always coming back for more. Companies with high trust cultures will always have lower turnover because employees don't want to risk going somewhere else for a few extra dollars an hour just to be miserable for the eight or more hours they're there every day. It's not worth it. And when employees do leave great workplace cultures, we often see them recommend others for those positions or come back at a later date. Trust is contagious, and people always want to be in spaces where it's present.

THE WAY LEADERS SHOW UP AND COMMUNICATE EVERY DAY IN THE WORKPLACE ULTIMATELY DECIDES THE ORGANIZATION'S CULTURE.

I have my suits custom-made by Singh Styles in Vancouver, Canada. When I purchase a suit for my speaking events, I am impressed with the craftsmanship, the personalization on the inside, and the collaboration process with designer Kam Bains. We have built a trusting relationship over the years. As a result, I'm less price-sensitive and willing to pay a little more for a suit tailored to my style and brand. Trust keeps me loyal to a business that isn't as convenient for my location but whose product I appreciate. Trust has caused me to refer more people to the business. Raving fans are always the best marketers for any company. And trust has made me more forgiving and patient when mistakes happen because I know they will always make it right. Singh Styles has created a trusting culture that keeps its customers coming back for more. Trust is their biggest competitive advantage, and it will always be yours, too.

Finally, Pat Summitt said, "Life is competitive. People are going to keep score. You cannot be afraid to go out and compete." I want all of you to go out in life and compete, but how you compete makes all the difference. Some people will go out and do whatever it takes to win at all costs. They will ruin relationships, run over people, and even sacrifice their integrity. Many might make it to the top, but they often stand there alone. That's because life without trust is lonely. It's never worth it. The other group of people will compete, but they will do it while still focusing on trust in the process. They honor their values and treat people kindly while still trying to win. You cannot lose when trust is your endgame, which is another reason trust is your biggest competitive advantage.

YOU CANNOT LOSE WHEN TRUST IS YOUR ENDGAME.

CHAPTER TWO
SUMMARY

- We all lose when we prioritize time over trust.
- Trust is money.
- We stop doing business with companies who break our trust.
- The best businesses will find a way to excel in balancing both time and trust.
- Trust is your biggest competitive advantage because it leads to:
  - Teamwork
  - Candor
  - Loyalty
  - Opportunity
- All relationships end when people become emotionally bankrupt.
- Your credibility as a leader is dependent on your ability to earn and keep people's trust.
- The way leaders show up and communicate every day in the workplace ultimately decides the organization's culture.
- Trust is your biggest competitive advantage because it keeps people coming back for more.
- You cannot lose when trust is your endgame.

YOUR ROAD TO YES!

CHAPTER THREE

SILENCE IS YOUR BIGGEST THREAT

Speak up. Own your voice.
What you have to say matters.
Silence serves no one.

If trust is your biggest competitive advantage, then silence is your biggest threat.

I recently had two friends go through a "friendship divorce." They had been best friends for years and knew the most vulnerable parts of each other's lives. They traveled together, owned a home together, and were there for the most challenging and joyful aspects of each other's lives. I thought they were inseparable. However, their priorities and vision for the future started to change somewhere along the way. Instead of talking about it, they stayed silent. The silence festered into resentment, and by the time it all came out, the damage was done. Each conversation led to an argument where both people were just trying to be right. They started to weaponize each other's pasts. Their actions became petty. Lawyers got involved, and each felt the other had manipulated the truth to fit the desired narrative. All the trust they had built over those years was shredded, doused in gasoline, and then lit on fire. The relationship was over. There was no going back.

All relationships can handle the truth. What they can't handle are silence and secrecy. Silence and secrecy are the enemies of trust. Mistrust generally starts with silence. People stop sharing their feelings and needs. Their silence bubbles into resentment, and when they finally talk, their intensity gets the best of them. Everyone loses when effective communication is superseded by ego.

SILENCE AND SECRECY ARE THE ENEMIES OF TRUST.

This type of behavior happens in organizations every day. Employees stop opening up and sharing with their managers. Managers stop investing and having the conversations they need to with their employees. Peers create transactional relationships where they only talk to each other when necessary. It doesn't take academic research to know what happens when there is silence and mistrust in a relationship. You become less engaged, slower to respond, skeptical of other people's thoughts and ideas, and more likely to start looking out only for yourself.

There are three reasons why people generally stay silent in relationships:

1. Lack of confidence
2. Climate of fear
3. Emotional exhaustion

LACK OF CONFIDENCE

A lack of confidence will keep people silent and playing smaller than their potential. I've always taught others, "Find your voice, and you will find your confidence." Our voice is directly connected to what we believe about ourselves and whether we feel our voice is worthy of being heard. In my book *Unleashing Potential*, I share that "Confidence is having the courage to show up as yourself and for yourself—even when that choice is risky, uncomfortable, or even scary." People who lack confidence in a relationship find it much harder to speak up and share their point of view.

If you lack confidence, you owe it to yourself to find your voice. Finding your voice doesn't require permission from anyone else. Confidence is putting the need to like yourself over the need to be liked by others. It's a decision, rooted in personal power, to focus on what you can control. It's choosing to let go of the fear of how someone receives the message and how they will respond, instead taking complete responsibility for how you deliver the message. Below are some tangible actions you can take to rediscover your voice and develop stronger confidence:

- Speak up when a restaurant gets your order wrong.
- Express your idea in a meeting (and then be okay if they don't want to move forward with it).
- Share your feelings when it's necessary to move the relationship forward.
- Say no to things you don't want to do.
- Show your appreciation for others.

If you're in a relationship with someone who lacks confidence, you don't have to own that for them; however, you can ensure you're doing what you can to create a climate of safety so that person feels safe enough to share their voice.

If you're leading someone on your team who lacks confidence, it's your job as a leader to provide coaching to that individual. Ask empowering questions that help them think differently about who they are. I often hear executive leaders say they encourage and want others in the organization to speak up. However, those leaders assume others have as much confidence to push back as they do. Many individuals in lower positions distort their message as they communicate up the organization.

Have the individuals set small, weekly steps they will take to speak up and share their perspectives. Check in with them and ask how it went, what they learned about themselves, and how it made them feel. When you change what people believe about themselves, you change how they show up in the world.

Finding your voice is a journey. Sometimes you get it right, and other times you get it wrong. Celebrate the moments that go well and give yourself a break when you feel you could have done better. It takes both experiences to learn and master your authentic voice. And the truth is, we never stop discovering the power of our voice.

CLIMATE OF FEAR

An environment of safety is directly correlated to trust, and without a sense of security, you're less likely to take a risk and speak up. When an individual's intensity intimidates other people out of their best thinking and acting, they create a climate of fear.

Below are some examples of how someone's intensity intimidates others:

- Cutting people off and talking over them
- Giving ultimatums
- Belittling one's competence or sense of identity

- Asking passive-aggressive questions like, "You know that's ridiculous, right?"
- Using silence as controlling behavior to get what you want
- Challenging someone in front of others
- Making comments that lack tact

Individuals who create a climate of fear will often justify their behavior by saying they're just a "truth-teller" and "don't beat around the bush." In those moments, they're just a jerk, and they sacrifice relationships for the need to be right.

In the movie *Whiplash*, Terence Fletcher is a music instructor known for his fear-based teaching style. His presence is both intimidating and explosive. He believes this approach is the way to bring out the best in others. Andrew Neiman is an aspiring jazz drummer who finds himself under the guise of Fletcher's "leadership." One minute, things will seem to be going well, and the next minute Andrew has a chair hurled at his head. Fletcher gets in his face and smacks him repeatedly until he can articulate if he is rushing or dragging. This behavior intimidates not only Andrew but everyone else in the band. This authoritative style is all Terence knows. As a result, he gets people to comply with his demands and improve their skills, but he crushes their spirit and self-worth. The people under him are always left to ask themselves, "Is it really worth all this?"

I had a coach once tell me that in every relationship, there are three people: you, the other person, and "the relationship." Both people create a dynamic very early on in the relationship based on how they communicate and the boundaries they do or don't set. That dynamic then shapes how people show up in the relationship moving forward. You owe it to yourself and the relationship to speak up at the first moment someone tries to intimidate you out of your best thinking. When you let it slide, you unconsciously teach the other person that they can continue to treat you like this in the relationship, and they will. Your power always lies in your choices, and no one should ever make you feel that you don't have a choice in the matter. You do.

YOUR ROAD TO YES!

Every organization has a responsibility to its employees to create an environment of psychological safety. If specific leaders hold team members mentally hostage, then those leaders should be fired. Organizations must do whatever is necessary to create a space where psychological safety is the norm. Speaking up and sharing your truth must be the expectation in organizations. They must be rewarded. Only then will you get the best ideas, minimize risks, and create a thriving culture founded on candor and care.

EXHAUSTED AND HAD ENOUGH

One of the biggest reasons people stay silent in a relationship is that they're exhausted and have had enough. They've tried speaking up multiple times in the past, but they were dismissed and shut down, or nothing changed. They've decided it's safer and more peaceful to keep their thoughts to themselves than to exert any more mental and emotional energy on the other person. When this happens, they abandon the relationship to protect themselves. This is how so many people feel when they're in a relationship but still feel alone.

I coached a mid-level manager who was struggling in the relationship with her boss. Her peers admired and respected her, but the boss's feedback did not mirror that. When I talked with the boss and shared the disconnect in perspectives, she acknowledged she had not been coaching or having the performance conversations she needed to have. Ironically, the employee was eventually put on a performance improvement plan and felt blindsided by her boss since there had not been much coaching leading up to that point. The trust between the two had eroded to a point where they were both being civil in their dialogue but weren't telling each other the truth or having the conversations they needed to repair the relationship. The silence only deepened the fault line. The employee eventually had enough. She was tired of trying to tip-toe around a boss who wasn't willing to put in the same effort. She left the organization.

> EVERYONE LOSES WHEN WE CONTINUOUSLY STAY SILENT ON THE THINGS THAT MATTER IN THE RELATIONSHIP.

Everyone loses when we continuously stay silent on the things that matter in the relationship. If we're in a relationship where we're exhausted and have had enough, we need to make choices to regain the feeling we want to have in healthy relationships. If we're exhausting people, we need to apologize, acknowledge that we didn't realize how our behavior was coming across, and ask the other person what they need from this relationship moving forward. Only then can we slowly begin to earn back an emotionally exhausted person's trust.

WHEN SILENCE IS APPROPRIATE

Silence is your biggest threat in a relationship when you use it as a coping mechanism or as a tool to manipulate others. However, there are specific moments when silence can serve you. Use silence when you need to keep your intensity in check, when what you have to say isn't going to move the relationship forward, or when you just need to listen.

IF WHAT YOU'RE ABOUT TO SAY WILL NOT MOVE THE RELATIONSHIP OR THE BUSINESS FORWARD, IT'S BEST TO STAY SILENT.

If your emotions are bubbling up and you know you're about to blow up, then it's always best to stay silent or let someone know that you need to step back until you can respond in a way that would serve the relationship. Silence often helps you get back to rational thinking and keep your character intact. My rule is that silence is better than being an ass. If what you're about to say will not move the relationship or the business forward, it's best to stay silent.

I had a boss who once told me that I needed to pick my hill to die on. She wasn't discouraging me from speaking up. In fact, she was encouraging the opposite. She believed in me and the perspective I brought. She helped me realize that I exhaust people and say a lot of nothing just to hear myself talk, whether I'm rephrasing what other people said or putting people on trial for any idea different from mine. She challenged me to think through why I felt the need to speak up and instead be more strategic with those moments. Her insight helped me shape my voice to communicate with more influence and gravitas.

Listening is one of the most challenging skills to master because it requires us to sit silently in the moment with someone versus thinking ahead and trying to fix their situation. We're often so consumed with jumping in with our perspective that we never hear what's being said. Learning to be an active listener teaches us that our biggest value is often not having the answer but rather making others feel less alone as they work through the problem themselves. Silence allows people to think for themselves, examine their thoughts and beliefs, and feel unconditionally supported and safe in that space. That's the power our silence can have when we use it purposefully.

Sometimes, especially in group situations, silence is initially best. It allows us to gather more information, demonstrate our collaborative nature, and take people with us through the process. If my initial thought is, "What on earth is this person talking about?" I need to stay silent, stop judging, and engage my curiosity more. It's only then that I have the potential to learn, see both myself and the other person differently, and eventually respond thoughtfully. I'm not going to lie—it's hard, and I'm not always successful. But silence has served me more in these situations than a judgmental or passive-aggressive response ever did.

THE REMEDY TO SILENCE

Silence is your biggest threat in a relationship, and the remedy is honest communication. If you feel icky and unsettled because of what someone did or what you did to someone else, then love and respect the relationship enough to tell the truth. Sometimes we must sour the immediate moment in the hope of having a better future together.

I often ask myself, "Can I move forward without addressing this issue and still be as

SILENCE IS YOUR BIGGEST THREAT IN A RELATIONSHIP, AND THE REMEDY IS HONEST COMMUNICATION.

kind and loving, both to myself and the other person?" If the answer is no, then I address the issue. Not addressing it would make me resentful, and I know I would slowly start pulling back from the relationship. If the answer is yes, then I acknowledge my feelings at that moment and remind myself that this one instance does not define the entire relationship.

Do not allow your silence to become a symbol of approval. The person you hurt is yourself every time you tip-toe around your feelings, avoid saying the things you need to say, or violate your boundaries. You have the right to honor your values. You have the right to say how something makes you feel. You have the right not to give people permission for their bad behavior. Yes, you are worth that choice!

CHAPTER THREE
SUMMARY

- Silence and secrecy are the enemies of trust.

- Everyone loses when effective communication is replaced with ego.

- There are three reasons why people generally stay silent in relationships:
  - Lack of confidence
  - Climate of fear
  - Emotional exhaustion

- Everyone loses when we continuously stay silent on the things that matter in the relationship.

- If what you're about to say will not move the relationship or the business forward, it's best to stay silent.

- Silence is your biggest threat in a relationship, and the remedy is honest communication.

- When deciding whether to speak up or stay silent, ask yourself: Can I move forward without addressing this issue and still be as kind and loving, both to myself and the other person?

CHAPTER FOUR

BUILDING TRUST IN YOURSELF

Healthy partnerships
Will never require you to
Forget who you are.

YOUR ROAD TO YES!

A man once came up to me after a keynote presentation I gave on trust. He cautiously shook my hand, looked directly at me, and said, "I have to tell you that I almost walked out of your talk."

"It was that good?" I joked.

He said the topic was hitting too close to home, forcing him to look at some things he had been avoiding. He got emotional. We talked about how he gives his trust away so freely and doesn't set boundaries or honor himself when people consistently break it. We discussed that building trust is both a head and heart process. We must extend trust to others (heart), but it's equally important that we pay attention to what people do with that trust and respond accordingly (head).

He acknowledged that he regularly sacrifices his self-trust in his desire to be loved. He's not alone. At some point in our lives, many of us have sacrificed ourselves for a brash boss, an employee who misused our kindness, an overbearing client, or someone we love. The thing that all these scenarios have in common is the fear of loss. We're so afraid of losing the job, the employee we feel we need, the client who brings in a lot of money, or the company of someone we love that we sacrifice ourselves. We always lose trust in ourselves when we're more concerned about losing others. It's never worth it because the people we keep get a second-rate version of us.

WE ALWAYS LOSE TRUST IN OURSELVES WHEN WE'RE MORE CONCERNED ABOUT LOSING OTHERS.

Healthy relationships never require you to sacrifice yourself repeatedly. You should never have to give up trust in yourself for trust in someone else. If you do, you're in the wrong relationship. If you ever need to choose between building trust with yourself or with someone else, always choose yourself. When you sacrifice your self-trust in a relationship, you:

IF YOU EVER NEED TO CHOOSE BETWEEN BUILDING TRUST WITH YOURSELF OR WITH SOMEONE ELSE, ALWAYS CHOOSE YOURSELF.

- Create a pattern of putting other's needs above your own
- Stop speaking up on the things that are important to you
- Grow slowly and methodically resentful
- Forget who you are

You always show up better in relationships when you have healthy levels of self-trust. And here's the good news: healthy relationships will never require you to choose between the two.

He ended our conversation by saying, "I'm glad I stayed." I responded, "I'm glad you stayed, too."

WHAT IS SELF-TRUST & WHY IS IT IMPORTANT?

In my workbook, *Unleashing Potential: Confidence,* I shared, "There is nothing more important in this world than your belief in yourself. What you believe or don't believe about yourself becomes the filter for how you show up in the world, how you make decisions, and how you treat yourself and others. Confidence is about putting the need to like yourself over the need to be liked by others. It is not being egocentric without any care of what other people think. Confident people do care about others, and they value what others think. They do not, however, wear those thoughts and feedback on their soul as signs of their worthiness."

Confidence comes from the Latin verb *fidere,* which means "to trust." Therefore, self-confidence is our ability to trust in ourselves and our ability to succeed. I use the terms "self-trust" and "self-confidence" interchangeably for this reason.

Self-trust is a clear and unwavering commitment to having your own back, not because other people aren't there for you, but because you understand where your power comes from. Self-trust is not about having all the answers or proving yourself to anyone else. It's an unequivocal understanding that you will persevere through whatever comes your way.

Self-trust is rooted in both conviction and clarity. You are clear about your authentic self, and you have the conviction to let yourself be seen. You understand that there is a time to let others have the spotlight, but you're just as willing to step into it (even if nervously) and add your perspective to the world. There will be plenty of situations where you find your self-trust waning. That's okay! Those are the moments you must call on your conviction. Conviction does not require comfort. It only requires that you believe in something so deeply that you're willing to step into the arena of discomfort and make your stance known. When we act on conviction, we gain even stronger clarity about who we are and what we stand for. We can then accept both the rewards and consequences of our decisions. As a result, conviction often leads to deeper levels of self-trust.

Self-trust is essential because self-trust changes how you see yourself. Coming out as gay was one of the most challenging moments in my life. I felt I was disappointing everyone around me. I often felt sick from the weight of the secret I was carrying, and I was afraid I would lose the people who said they loved me unconditionally. Coming out was an emotional process of stepping into the truth of who I was and then accepting the rewards and consequences of that decision. Now, over twenty years later, I realize we never stop "coming out," no matter who we are. We continue to discover new paths that lead us to more authentic versions of ourselves. We continue to learn how to accept and appreciate the parts of ourselves that we didn't like before. And we continue to make choices that honor the truth of who we are. Building self-trust is a coming-out process that is never finished. If we're lucky, we just continue to evolve how we see ourselves, and in that space, we learn to love ourselves more.

SELF-TRUST CHANGES HOW YOU SEE YOURSELF.

Self-trust shifts how other people see you. It is difficult for others to trust you when you don't even trust yourself. Self-doubt and constantly seeking validation don't cultivate confidence. *The Atlantic's* 2014 article, "The Confidence Gap," posed the question: "Is confidence just as important as competence?" The answer is yes: "Success, it turns out, correlates just as closely with confidence as it does with competence." The more confident leaders appeared, the more people perceived them as competent. The goal here is to help you develop a healthy, authentic level of self-trust. You show up differently when you believe in yourself and who you are. People can feel it, and most people will appreciate it.

SELF-TRUST CHANGES HOW YOU SHOW UP IN RELATIONSHIPS.

Self-trust changes how you show up in relationships. The relationship you have with yourself often mirrors your relationships with others. If doubt, fear, and criticism play a prominent role in your daily mindset, this will rub off on the other people in your life. You will project your insecurities onto them, dislike people for the very same behaviors you refuse to see in yourself, and use people in ways that make you feel pretty, successful, smart, and loved. When we lack self-trust, we often gravitate to pettiness, shaming, and believing we are right about everything. There's another way! When we build self-trust, we speak up more, set boundaries, see the other person as a partner versus a competitor, and do the inside work to make ourselves feel whole. As a result, we have better relationships.

Self-trust increases your resilience. Resiliency is about your ability to get up and move forward in the face of challenges. When you get knocked down and you have a high level of self-trust, you might complain, become mad or sad, or feel lost; however, you get back up quickly because you believe in yourself and what's to come. Self-trust helps us consciously decide to believe that even in the messiness of our lives, things are lining up in our favor. Alan Cohen has a quote I love that says, "Use pain as a stepping stone, not a campground." Self-trust helps pull us out of the campground mentality. It gives us the vision to look back and remember all the times we did get back up and took a step forward. And because we did it then, we have the fortitude and skill to do it again. And so we do.

Self-trust boosts your level of optimism. Taylor Swift said, "Happiness and confidence are the prettiest things you can wear." The good news is that numerous research studies confirm a correlation between higher confidence and greater levels of happiness, particularly for those in Western civilization. That doesn't mean these individuals walk around perpetually chipper. However, they find happiness in where they are today, reaching within to discover their value, and working towards goals that make them feel alive.

SELF-TRUST BOOSTS YOUR LEVEL OF OPTIMISM.

Before teaching a workshop on trust, I have people respond to a short survey so I can weave their answers into the program. One of the questions I ask participants is to tell me one piece of advice they'd recommend to a good friend struggling with self-trust. Most of the responses are a version of "I'd tell them to just believe in themselves." They give this advice with good intentions, but if their struggling friend naturally knew how to believe in themselves, they would do so. Since they don't, they're left to interpret what that means. Individuals who lack self-trust need tangible and specific actions they can experiment with over time.

Below is a list of ten actions that will help someone build strong self-trust:

1. Honor Who You Are
2. Act Like You Belong
3. Grow Your Professional Competence
4. Speak Up
5. Take Ownership of Your Feelings
6. Go on an "Advice Detox"
7. Practice Forgiveness
8. Believe in Something Bigger Than Yourself
9. Get Yourself an Army
10. Take Action

This is not an exhaustive list of every strategy, but it's a good start. These actions are grounded in emotional intelligence competencies and designed to help you think differently about yourself, your voice, your presence, and your choices. My hope is they help you or someone you know. At your core, you are full of insightful wisdom, remarkable fortitude, and unshakable confidence. That's the truth of who you are. Now, let's help you believe that about yourself by looking at each of these actions in more detail.

HONOR WHO YOU ARE

Every decision you make stems from what you think you are and represents the value that you put upon yourself.

— *A Course in Miracles*

The core of our self-worth and self-trust are rooted in what and who we believe we are. When we don't have a clear vision of who we are at our best, we rely on other people to tell us. That's problematic. We build our identity off their words and then wake up one day only to realize that's not who we are at all. Then we feel lost, and we're back on a journey to find ourselves again. Another reason it's problematic is that it shifts ownership. We allow others to have more stock in our minds, and then we build an unstable foundation based on their glimpses. We deserve more stability, and the only person who can provide that is ourselves. If we want to change how we feel about ourselves and how we show up in the world, we must change our beliefs about who we are.

Try this exercise:

1. Recall a time in your life when you feel you showed up at your best and were proud of your presence (personally or professionally).
2. Identify the top three traits you demonstrated that allowed you to show up your best (i.e., confidence, empathy, kindness, preparation, mindfulness).
3. For each of your three words, briefly describe the actions you would demonstrate if you were living that word out fully.
4. How well are you doing at these actions in your daily life?

5. What impact would it have on yourself and your relationships if you focused on showing up more from this space?
6. How does this vision of who you are at your best change or reinforce what you believe about yourself?

You learn to see yourself more clearly when you dare to answer, "Who am I when I'm at my best?" When you do this work, you will no longer need to rely on others' validation to see you. You show up more authentically. As a result, you feel more confident. It's the type of confidence that isn't loud or boisterous. It's quiet. Unassuming. And impactful. And because you see yourself, you create the space for other people to be seen, too.

Actress and model Dominique Jackson once said, "I stopped looking for acceptance when I actually found myself. My life is not for someone else to accept." Self-trust is standing up for the truth of who you are every damn day—regardless of whether other people acknowledge, appreciate, or accept it. You do not build self-trust by conforming. You build self-trust by embracing your unique, authentic self. And here's the good news: you don't have to change who you are. You've always been that person. You might have forgotten it or temporarily walked away from it, but that vision has always been there. All you need to do is step back into the truth of who you've always been and live it out every day. Trust in that!

ACT LIKE YOU BELONG

I've ruined relationships in my past because of my need to be right. In my mindset, I had spent a lifetime defining my self-worth through my knowledge; therefore, I felt I had to protect it at all costs. What would it mean if I was wrong? Who was I without my answers? What would people see if they saw beneath my facade of confidence? The truth is, we all become addicted to something. I was addicted to proving myself, not to the world but to myself. Unfortunately, other people were the ones who experienced the consequences of my actions. I sacrificed intimacy for transactions. I abandoned empathy for tactless assertiveness. I eroded trust because I justified my bad behavior as "truth-telling." I now realize that I fought so hard to be seen and heard that other people became invisible, and when people become invisible to someone, they will simply find someone else who sees them for who they want to be. In that journey, I had forgotten the truth of who I was when I was at my best. I wasn't living a life based on my truth. I was living a life based on trauma, ineffective coping strategies, and the constant need to prove myself. It wasn't until I stopped trying to prove myself to the world that I learned to trust myself.

The most impactful leadership advice I've ever received came from Greg Creed, the former CEO of Taco Bell and Yum! Brands. When asked what one piece of leadership advice he would give to others, he said, "Stop trying to prove you belong and act like you belong." Acting like we belong means we show up in spaces honoring who we already are and have always been. That doesn't require a performance. Proving yourself is a performance to see if you can win people over with your thoughts, feelings, and ideas. It sometimes causes us to act inauthentically or push back in ways we usually wouldn't. Every meeting becomes a lifetime performance, and you're constantly auditioning for your Oscar nomination. Sometimes it works, but most times, people read right through it. Regardless, it's exhausting. Acting like you belong requires a different kind of effort because you're walking into spaces authentically. You're not consumed by how you think you need to show up based on others' expectations. You recognize that your value is in your presence and the energy you bring into a room. You're not concerned with being the smartest person or speaking just to be heard. Your quiet confidence allows you to show up less stressed, think more clearly, articulate your perspective, and detach from the outcome. You recognize that everyone does not demonstrate this level of authenticity. It is your strength. Thus, a question to ask yourself before walking into any space is, "How would I show up if I was acting like I belonged and not focused on trying to prove I belonged?"

> STOP TRYING TO PROVE YOU BELONG AND ACT LIKE YOU BELONG.

Early in my corporate career, I was given a chance to travel the country to train people on a new healthcare product a company was rolling out. I ended up speaking at several cities in Texas. While there, I wore a wedding band, despite the fact that I wasn't even dating someone. It was before gay marriage had been legalized. I naively believed that maybe the wedding band would throw people off and make my sexual orientation a non-issue. *Come on, y'all.* I look back now, and though I'm shocked that I even thought that, I acknowledge that I did it to try and fit in, avoid criticism, and be liked. I was caught up with proving I belonged instead of walking into that room and acting like I belonged. Over time, by building stronger self-trust, I now refuse to own other people's insecurities. I've accepted that other people's judgments and assumptions have nothing to do with me, and I don't have to take them on. Those aren't my people, and I'm not going to cater to their insecurities. And neither should you.

We learn to succeed by being exactly who we are, not playing a part. While speaking at an NCAA event in 2022, someone asked me if I ever get nervous when talking to people anymore. I told them, "Not really. I might get butterflies because of my excitement, but it's not rooted in fear. I learned to manage my nerves, anxiousness, and fear when I stopped hustling for others' validation." Do I want the audience to like and resonate with my message? Of course. Do I want people to leave feeling inspired and ready to take action? Yes! But that's about them and how they show up in the space. I can't own that for them. What I can do is show up and deliver my message in the most authentic way possible with their needs and concerns at the forefront. That's my responsibility. It's not for them to like me as a person. In fact, some of my most powerful messages challenge who we are and how we show up. When we are in spaces where we're trying to prove ourselves, we always respond out of fear of not being liked or seen as good enough. We hustle for the person to think we're smart enough, capable enough, pretty enough, loveable enough, or talented enough. You might wait a lifetime for others to see your worth, and in the waiting, give up your inner peace and belief in yourself. It's never worth it!

Will you ever be in spaces where someone in the room might not think you're good enough because of your age, gender, race, sexual orientation, religion, or appearance? Unfortunately, you probably will. But owning that narrative doesn't serve you. That's about them and their insecurity. I had to stop seeing those factors as things that could hold me back. Instead, acting like I belonged allowed me to shift my mindset and realize that I bring a unique point of view into the room. Trust that the universe is constantly putting you in spaces where you can honor the truth of who you are.

Self-trust is your ability to love yourself without conditions. There are enough people in life who place conditions on your being. You shouldn't be one of them. You have nothing to prove. As Rita Mae Brown once said, "The reward for conformity is that everyone likes you but yourself."

GROW YOUR PROFESSIONAL COMPETENCE

Years ago, I was sitting in a Starbucks in Louisville, Kentucky, meeting with an executive from Fifth Third Bank. He set his coffee down and asked, "What do you want to be an expert in?" No one had ever asked me that question before or since. Before that question, I never thought of myself as an "expert" or entertained the possibility of being one in the future. He elaborated, "When a company like ours has a problem, we want to go to the expert. What are we coming to you for in the future?" The question challenged me to think more deeply and dream more audaciously. This leader knew that, without a clear answer, I couldn't align my development in a meaningful direction. He also understood that as I grow my knowledge in an area, I trust myself more. As a result, others begin to trust me more, too.

Many of us have never acknowledged ourselves as experts in an area. Maybe it makes us feel self-centered, or perhaps it's because we don't know the next right step in making it happen. Working on becoming an expert is not about believing you have all the answers. It means learning as much as you can on a specific topic you feel passionate about and using your voice to contribute to the conversation.

YOUR ROAD TO YES!

There is a lot of scholarly research on how confidence helps you come across as confident. However, I don't want others to only perceive you as confident. I want you to believe it, feel it. And for most of you reading this, you or someone you lead might already struggle with the confidence piece. So, we're going to focus on growing our competence as a tactic to help us build more confidence.

After the executive from Fifth Third asked me what I wanted to be an expert in, I went home and reflected on that question. I finally decided body language was the area I was going to own. I didn't need to be the world's most renowned person on the topic, but I wanted to commit to knowing it better than others in the spaces where I worked and taught. I read all the books I could on the topic. I received a certification from The Body Language Institute taught by former FBI agent and body language expert Janine Driver. I decided my take on the topic would not be how to read others' body language or detect if people are lying. That's the area of focus for most law enforcement specialists. Instead, my focus would be on effective communication and how to use body language to connect with others. I started delivering keynotes and workshops on the topic. The more I delivered them, the more positive feedback I received. Eventually, people started giving me more opportunities. Over time, body language evolved into emotional intelligence, then into coaching, and now into leadership presence and how to communicate in ways that build trust. As I committed to growing my competence, my belief in myself and the value I bring grew. And so will yours!

Answer this question: "What topic do I want to be an expert in?" I've worked with individuals who have given such diverse answers as engineering, instructional design, strategic thinking, relationship building, and economic development. It doesn't matter what topic you choose, as long as you choose. If you select a topic unrelated to what you're doing now, kudos to you for being honest with yourself. You now get to decide if you want to put a plan in place to pursue that passion. Having a clear vision will always help pull you forward.

Now that you have a clear answer, you're ready to take action and build your competence. Below are ten easy ways you can do so over the next few weeks:

- Read the top books on that subject matter.
- Subscribe to relevant blogs and newsletters.
- Listen to podcasts.
- Establish "mastermind" relationships with like-minded people.
- Earn a certification.
- Attend a conference or webinar.
- Join a professional association.
- Complete an eLearning course.
- Ask for relevant stretch projects at work.
- Post about the topic on social media.

The more you grow your professional competence, the more of an asset you become to your boss, the organization, and ultimately the customers you serve. Hopefully, the organization values and recognizes the expertise you bring. If they don't, here's the good news: you've built your skillset up enough to where you're very desirable to other employers. You never have to feel like someone is holding you hostage.

Finally, remember to give yourself permission to elevate and expand your area of expertise over the years. You're not committed to this one answer forever. It's just the next right answer in your journey. Confidence comes when you take action, get results, are recognized for your contributions, and receive more opportunities. Slowly, you'll start to see yourself the way others have always seen you: knowledgeable and talented.

SPEAK UP

I once coached a client who was working on developing stronger self-trust. We discussed how confidence is directly connected to our voice. Some people believe, "Oh, I'll speak up once I feel confident." I tell them, "It doesn't work that way, boo. You wait for that day, and you'll never speak up." Self-trust is choosing to believe that what you have to say is just as valuable as someone else's thoughts and experiences and that you owe it to both yourself and the relationship to speak up. Owning your voice isn't some straight-line path where you always get it right every time. You will have off-days. You will say something and be like, "Damn, I wish I would have said that differently." But you're going to have more days when you're proud of yourself. You will walk out of a meeting knowing you shared your perspective. You will learn to say no, set boundaries, and ask for what you want. More importantly, you will feel proud because you committed yourself never to be the person who silences you.

People-pleasers are the biggest culprits when it comes to those who silence themselves. I've coached several chronic people-pleasers who never spoke up because they were afraid of how it would make the other person feel. They were more concerned with being liked than being heard. It cost them their self-trust. You always lose if trust in a relationship is only based on the other person's view of you. When this happens, you'll placate to others' emotions. You'll find yourself tiptoeing around for their approval. But you're not a ballet dancer, and your feet are tired. You can stop. You don't have to give up your truth to make other people more comfortable. Trust isn't about making people comfortable all the time. You owe it to the relationship to speak up, share your thoughts, and ask for what you want. It doesn't mean you'll always get your way or that everyone will agree with you. But they'll know where you stand, and I believe they'll respect you more. More importantly, you'll respect yourself more.

I once worked with a client whose goal was to be more comfortable expressing differing opinions. I could tell she was leaning into this week over week and rediscovering the power of her voice. During one of our sessions, I asked her, "I've witnessed your progress on this. What was the change?" She stated, "I now understand their disagreement isn't about me, and I don't have to wear their feedback on my soul." I could have cried. Her insight is a reminder that you are not responsible for how other people feel. You are responsible for how you deliver the message. People are dragging a lifetime of baggage behind them, and they are filtering everything you say through their baggage, values, and energy. You can't try to control how your message lands with someone. What you can do is share your thoughts in the most authentic, non-judgmental way possible. It's freeing when you realize that you don't have to own someone else's reaction or hang their feedback on your soul.

Your voice is directly connected with your self-trust. If you're someone who has stopped speaking up for themselves, then the goal is for you to start. Below are a few ways you can speak up in small everyday moments:

- Express how your day is really going.
- Tell someone when you're ready to leave.
- Explain what you need from someone.
- Let the waiter know if your order is wrong.
- Ask for help when you need it.
- Say "no" and explain why if it doesn't feel right.
- Share your thoughts in a meeting.
- Recognize someone's efforts.

People can't trust someone they do not know. The only way people get to know you is when you express yourself. When we stay silent on things that matter, we can come across as emotionally detached and that we don't care. Self-trust blooms when you allow others to see you. One of the most fundamental ways you can do that is by speaking up.

TAKE OWNERSHIP OF YOUR FEELINGS

Part of building self-trust is taking full ownership of your feelings. Although you don't have the right to take hurtful action based on your feelings, you certainly do have the right to acknowledge and talk about whatever you feel. All emotions serve a purpose. When we're more in tune with our emotions, we become more in tune with ourselves and the relationships in our lives. Emotions teach us about our triggers, intuition, mindset, and needs.

In season one, episode six of the Netflix series *Barbarians*, during the heat of battle, one of the main characters says, "We can only win when we're in complete control of our feelings." When we lose awareness and control of our emotions, we stop thinking authentically, logically, and strategically. We allow ourselves to get emotionally hijacked and react in ways unbecoming of our highest self. We let fear take root, and it engulfs everything in its path. When the fire is finally extinguished, we might still be standing, but we have lost the battle, for lying in the charred remains is a little bit of our soul. We can't take back what was said. We can't undo the pain it caused. We are all damaged. We have all lost. Taking full ownership of our feelings and responding to those feelings is how we save ourselves, help others save themselves, and learn to trust each other.

I once had a client who kept telling me she wasn't an assertive person but wanted to learn. As we dove into her patterns of behavior, we discovered she doesn't speak up because she's too concerned with how the other person is going to feel. She stopped giving up her truth to make other people more comfortable. As a result, she sacrificed her voice and belief that both people could handle whatever truth she shared. I asked her, "What would change if you stopped trying to own their feelings for them?" That was the aha! moment for her. She recognized that trying to prevent someone else from experiencing certain feelings is a form of control, and that's not how she wanted to show up in the relationship. She needed to allow the other person to feel whatever they were going to feel and express that, so they could learn and decide how to move forward together. Others' feelings are not yours to own, but you are one hundred percent responsible for how you deliver your message. Other people's reactions are their choice, and when you stop trying to own their reactions for them, you free yourself up to acknowledge and focus on yours. In doing so, you learn to trust what you're feeling.

OTHERS' FEELINGS ARE NOT YOURS TO OWN.

When you take ownership of your feelings, you're better able to identify when you're no longer showing up your best. There are times when I catch myself curtly responding to emails, not being present for people, and doing work but not being productive. I can tell my energy is off. Sometimes I describe the feeling as "icky." Other times I identify that emotion as tired, overwhelmed, or just plain bored. Taking ownership of that feeling does not mean I just acknowledge it and keep plugging along. That doesn't serve me, nor the people I will encounter throughout the day. Ownership would be to recognize the emotion and then take some action that would allow me to reconnect to my best self.

I was once in a meeting about the COVID pandemic when an executive said, "The past eighteen months have been difficult. *We're emotionally wrecked.*" So many leaders have worked so tirelessly through the pandemic, trying to motivate others, that now they're emotionally depleted. Heck, I'd say almost every parent feels the same emotions. Trying to shut those emotions off and ignore them while continuing along is not effective. That's not taking ownership. That's avoidance. We do not honor ourselves and build self-trust by avoiding and ignoring our experiences. When we don't create habits that allow us to emotionally detox, we drag that "wreck" home. Unfortunately, the people we love the most get the worst of us. Then we're right back at work in a cycle of survival. That's not a successful strategy for any person or business, and it's never going to create a workplace culture that brings out the best in everyone. Remember the quote from *Barbarians*: "We can only win when we're in complete control of our feelings."

Being in control of your feelings starts with recognizing the emotions you're feeling. Get good at saying to yourself, "I feel _____." I'm going to challenge you to avoid just using words like "happy" or "mad." Those are surface-level physical reactions, but there's usually a deeper emotion underneath them. Peel back the layers and see if you can identify what's causing those feelings. More importantly, when you're aware that you're not in a great space, it's your responsibility to take action and get recentered.

Below are eight emotional recharge habits that we can all do in twenty minutes or less. These actions allow you to shift your focus, reconnect with yourself, and/or release endorphins. Pick one or two that you'd be willing to experiment with over the next couple of weeks and see how they work for you:

YOUR ROAD TO YES!

1. Engage in a bit of physical activity.
2. Take a creativity break.
3. Identify five things you're grateful for.
4. Watch something funny.
5. Meditate or pray.
6. Reflect on what went well today.
7. Listen to feel-good music.
8. Recognize someone else.

It's hard to know you need to recharge when you're not in full awareness or control of your feelings. I hope you'll start to see your emotions as a strength and an asset in your life, not as something that should be avoided or silenced. You are cosmically wired with the gift of intuition. Taking ownership of your emotions is one way you learn to trust that gift and yourself. You cannot show up well for anyone when you're emotionally bankrupt. The people and organizations worth your time and effort don't want a second-rate version of you. They want you at your best, which will require you to implement effective emotional recharge habits. Taking a break and recharging should be the norm, not the last straw.

GO ON AN ADVICE DETOX

When we lack self-trust, we often outsource our decision-making because we put more value in others' opinions than we do our own. We ask everyone else what we should do with our career, relationships, and daily challenges, and then we feel perplexed when they think we should do something that doesn't align with our original choice. When we outsource our decision-making long enough, we stop listening to our intuition and trusting that we are the only person who knows what is best for us. As a certified coach, I never give people answers because there is no one right answer or one right path for anything. We in the coaching industry believe that every person knows what is best for themselves. You can only empower people by helping them take accountability for their choices, accepting both the rewards and consequences that come as a result.

A detox is necessary when you want to remove anything unhealthy in your life, whether that's sugar, a controlled substance, or advice. Advice becomes unhealthy when you put more weight on other people's opinions than your own. That's why an advice detox is sometimes just the thing to help you learn how to trust yourself a little more. Set a period (i.e., a week, a month) where you don't ask anyone else for their advice on what choices you should make. It will require you to shut out all the noise around you and embrace uncertainty. It's risky, and you're going to feel nervous. That's okay. That's what it feels like to learn to trust yourself. You'll also want someone to tell you that it will turn out okay, but no person or solution can offer you that. Your job is to make the best choice with the information you currently have available. If new information arises, you have the freedom to adapt and change course.

Remember: you are never stuck! As someone who teaches leadership presence, I can tell you that nothing looks better on you than resiliency. Resiliency is always focused on "the next right answer." You have everything you need to make that choice for yourself. I wish I could promise you that the journey will be easy, that you'll never fall and be stuck…but just as I don't believe in toxic negativity, I also don't believe in toxic positivity. The truth is, unexpected things will happen, and you will continue to have regular moments of failure throughout the rest of your life, but resiliency is a choice all of us make in the face of that. It requires you to pick yourself up, learn with a renewed vision, and make another choice to move forward into possibility. That type of presence creates a legacy people never forget, and that's a legacy that changes lives. Everyone loves a good comeback story, and you're always just one choice away from having one yourself.

PRACTICE FORGIVENESS

There comes a moment in life where you realize you've hurt people. You've done things you're not proud of. You've acted in ways that twisted your stomach into knots, and the shame quickly followed. You felt as though the guilt would never go away. You spent mornings and nights holding yourself hostage to the actions that replayed in your mind because if you can feel guilt, if you can repeatedly punish yourself, then maybe—just maybe—the pain won't be there tomorrow. But it didn't work. So you resorted to burying it deep down. If you can forget about it, act like it hasn't taken up residence in your soul, and cover it up in the busyness of work, then you can survive another day. But shame doesn't let you have an off-day. It's always lurking, and it just causes you to run faster. You run so fast and so long that you end up losing yourself. It's usually only when we're so fatigued that we can't go any further that we finally surrender. We own our actions. We acknowledge the impact they had. We realize that was not the truth of who we are. And then we let it go and give ourselves a second chance. It is then that we find the miracle of forgiveness. And in the process, we find ourselves again.

In my book *Bold New You*, I write, "Forgiveness is a fundamental step in taking care of ourselves. It invites us to slow down, do the necessary gritty work to heal, and experience what it is like to navigate through life undistracted by all we see in the rearview mirror. Forgiveness can only happen in the present moment. When we offer forgiveness to ourselves or others, we make a conscious choice to experience life differently, walk taller and lighter in our truth, and write a different ending to our story. Forgiveness shifts us out of a victim mentality and empowers us to be a better leader of ourselves." Many people need to forgive themselves for who they were at a particular moment and what they did or did not do. Your lack of self-forgiveness erodes your self-trust because you tie your entire self to the person you were in that particular moment versus the person you are the rest of the time. Are you one of these people? If so, one of the most important questions you will ever ask yourself is, "What do I need to forgive myself for?"

I've always believed that shame and guilt are simply signals that we walked out on the truth of who we are. It's just information, not a life sentence. Researcher and bestselling author Brené Brown taught me that "shame cannot survive in silence." Therefore, the path to self-forgiveness starts by acknowledging and speaking about what happened. Sometimes the only person you need to say it to is yourself, while other times, it might help to talk to your best friend, a higher power, or the other person impacted by your actions.

Speaking our shame or guilt aloud prevents it from taking root and festering inside us. It is then that you start to feel lighter and less alone in the world. Keep speaking until you can authentically let it go.

Next, I would invite you to accept that you did the best you could when making those past decisions. That doesn't mean your actions were ethical, legal, or justified. It doesn't mean you lived out your values and who you believe you are most often. It means that you showed up based on the insecurities you felt in the moment, the emotions you were experiencing, and all the other factors that led to you behaving in a way you regret. You can acknowledge that this is not who you are at your highest self while still acknowledging that you weren't operating from that space at that moment. It doesn't give you a free pass, but it does offer you the chance to forgive a mistake.

Finally, when you're ready, write an apology letter to yourself. This isn't the moment to beat yourself up. You've done that long enough. Instead, it's a moment to be vulnerable, empathetic, and accountable. What does that version of you, who showed up at that moment where guilt and shame took root, need to hear? What advice would you give yourself now? What are you committing to do differently moving forward? The awareness you'll receive from writing the letter will support you as you heal.

Who you are—who all of us are—is built on mistakes and pain but rooted in love. Love challenges us not to emotionally disconnect, abandon the best part of who we are, and make the same mistakes repeatedly. Love is your declaration to the world that you are not a mess. You live in a messy world, and you are brave enough to feel through it and do the work you need to do to become a more authentic and loving you. Forgiving yourself is one of the most loving acts possible, and it helps you start to believe in yourself again.

BELIEVE IN SOMETHING BIGGER THAN YOU

I don't know what's beyond the clouds, whispering in the wind and guiding me from behind my shadow. But I know there's something bigger than me. I believe that. I have to. We grow cynical, cold, and

lonely in the absence of belief. I don't want to live a life tha
want to wake up, feel supported, and be inspired by the hope uiau
who I am and what I do is part of something bigger than I'll ever
know or understand. I want to trust in that, and so I do!

Believe in something that calls you to have more faith and hope. For
some people, it's believing in purpose. For others, it's their family, the
universe, a specific religion, nature, guardian angels, or miracles. It
doesn't matter what it is as long as you have something to believe in.

Optimism is one of the fifteen core emotional intelligence elements
based on the EQi 2.0 assessment I administer to clients. My
experience has proved that when people are low in that area, they
typically lack a belief in something bigger than themselves. Their
mindset is usually, "Well, this is as good as it will get, I guess." As
a result, they tend to lack resilience and stay in victimhood longer.
Oprah Winfrey talked about believing in something bigger than
herself and said, "Being fearless was being able to release my fears to
that which is greater than myself."

When you believe in something bigger than yourself, you release
yourself from understanding the present moment and give yourself
faith that it will work out. You lean on that belief and use it to help
pull you through both the good and hard times.

This concept helps build self-trust because it empowers you to make
decisions that keep you moving forward. It permits you not to have
all the answers, but trust that it will work out and everything will
align for a greater good.

Take a moment to answer these three questions:

1. What can you put your belief in to make you feel less
   alone in the world?
2. What significance does that relationship have in your
   life today?
3. What actions would help grow that relationship?

GET AN ARMY

I remember being on vacation with someone in my late thirties when he turned to me and said, "When are you going to let yourself be loved?" Wow. I paused to let that comment sink in, realizing he was right. I grew up with a deep desire to be independent, where I didn't have to rely on anyone to have my back. It served me well in some ways and held me back in others. It's hard to have intimacy or let others in when you always have one hand up, ready to catch yourself if the rug is yanked out from beneath you. Yes, building self-trust is learning how to have your back through life, but it doesn't require you to alienate others in the process.

We don't have to live life trying to protect ourselves. We build self-trust by knowing that we can go all-in and handle whatever comes our way. When we surrender the need to maneuver through life by ourselves, we invite the possibility of healthy relationships in our life. Healthy relationships are mutually satisfying, meaning they're a win-win for everyone involved. You need people who can champion your successes, be a truth-teller when you need to hear it, act as a sounding board when you need to vent, and rally the troops when you need support.

You need a small but mighty army! This army makes you feel less alone in the world. It acts as a mirror and teaches you about yourself, and the healthy relationships you develop inevitably increase your overall well-being.

Four key areas of your life where you will want to develop relationships include your family, your friends, your place of work, and your industry. For each, identify the people in that area who are currently part of your army, and then ask the following questions:

1. What areas need more time and attention?
2. What could you specifically do to develop relationships in those areas?
3. What would success look like in the next three months? One year?

Remember that meaningful relationships take time. The goal is not to feel we're putting in all the work, and it's not to detach altogether. It's the constant pushing and pulling of effort from both people. Remember, we all get busy and have different priorities at times. Give people some grace, check in with them regularly, be willing to share your honest thoughts, and engage in difficult conversations when you need to. It's all part of how you build trust.

Finally, there might come a day when you realize that someone is no longer the right person for your army. That's okay. Trust your intuition. You cannot accommodate people into a new way of thinking, and your lovability should never be predicated on people who place conditions on everyone in their life. You will find freedom when you stop investing in people who do not deserve your time and attention and stop giving the cynics in your life an audience. Take the time you waste trying to prove your lovability and spend it on people who already believe you are good enough just the way you are. The right people will always make you believe in yourself, too. That's your army!

TAKE ACTION

I once coached a client who was trying to figure out what he wanted to do with his life. During our time together, he criticized all the people in a specific field who had made it to the top. I observed, "You just sat here for five minutes and trashed every successful person you could think of while sitting at home on your couch with no job in that field. Where is that coming from?" Without hesitation, he stated, "Because it's easier to talk shit than do anything about it." That's the thing with just talking about taking action: it's not risky, so you don't have to accept the consequences. It lets you avoid the problems, but it also withholds the rewards, keeping you stuck where you are, slowly growing bitter and judgmental towards the people who pass you.

You learn to trust yourself by taking action, not sitting on the sidelines talking about it. The more you make decisions and feel like you're moving forward, the more you will believe in yourself. First, however, you must be willing to step on the court and give it a try!

> YOU LEARN TO TRUST YOURSELF BY TAKING ACTION, NOT SITTING ON THE SIDELINES TALKING ABOUT IT.

No one becomes a great player just sitting on the sidelines, playing Monday morning quarterback. They stepped in, threw the ball, missed, threw it again, and eventually scored more than they missed.

I know many people who have talked about success but never took the next step to make it happen. I bet you do, too. We bury our dreams in journals, conversations, and empty promises when we don't take action on them. That doesn't have to be your dream. Your dreams become a reality when you take consistent action.

I get that this can be scary. The fear of making the wrong choice often holds us back. But what if it's not about being wrong? What if it's simply about making the next choice? We might not know what to do a decade, year, or even month from now. But we always know what the next right answer for us is if we're listening to our intuition. You know right now if you need to invest more in a certain relationship, if you want to move up in your organization, or if it's time to leave and put your energy and talents elsewhere. You might not have all the details figured out or know every step in the journey. No one does. You're not supposed to. And even if you did, life would happen, and you'd probably have to adapt and change course anyway. Making the next right choice is choosing to take action and then permitting yourself to change when necessary.

I once coached another client who was trying to decide if she would stay at her job or make a move to another organization. She had been waiting for weeks for the new organization to provide her with information. She was stressed and in a constant state of flux. During one of our calls, she said, "I need them to tell me…." She paused. She realized she was waiting on other people to provide her the clarity she so desperately needed and wanted. "No," she quickly corrected herself. "I don't need them to tell me anything. I can make the decision and create my own clarity." YES. YES. YES. We build self-trust when we focus on the things we can control. Creating clarity and taking action in your life is at the heart of owning your power and believing in yourself. What action do you need to take?

EMOTIONAL INTELLIGENCE & SELF-TRUST

Getting certified in emotional intelligence and the EQi 2.0 assessment was a game-changer in my development and career. The assessment outlines the fifteen core traits of emotional intelligence and highlights how the traits are interconnected, shaping how we lead, love, and communicate in all areas of our lives.

Four elements significantly impact our overall well-being and happiness: self-regard, self-actualization, optimism, and interpersonal relationships. Self-regard deals with your confidence and how you view yourself. Self-actualization is your ability to set and go after realistic, meaningful goals. Optimism is maintaining a positive outlook in the face of adversity, and interpersonal relationships deal with forming and maintaining mutually satisfying relationships.

I share this with you because I believe these four elements are crucial to building trust in ourselves. I have seen that when my coaching clients become proficient in each of these areas, they:

- See themselves more favorably
- Learn, speak up, and go after what they want
- Build healthier relationships
- Become more resilient

Each of the ten actions I shared on building self-trust connects to at least one of these four emotional intelligence components, and often more. I'm not sure they're something we ever master, but they are skills we consistently work on, refine, and come to understand on deeper levels. And the deeper we go, the more we learn to believe in ourselves.

THE IMPORTANCE OF QUICK WINS

One of the quickest ways to start building self-trust is getting some quick wins. It's going to take some new habits to break some old patterns. When we try something new and receive positive results, we're more likely to continue doing it. That's because your trust equity increases with the more wins you garner. Therefore, I'm going to challenge you to complete the following exercise:

- Review the list of ten ways to build self-trust in yourself.
- Identify two areas that are your biggest opportunities.
- Commit to doing at least one concrete thing in those areas over the next week.

I know the way self-trust feels. There is a lightness in the way I walk, a directness in the way I speak, and a calmness in the energy I put out in the world. It's not that bullshit about "fake it 'till you make it," or "own the room," or "don't rely on anyone else." That's advice we receive from people still struggling to find themselves. I don't blame them. Learning to trust yourself is grueling. It requires you to go mining deeply in your soul, remember who you are, and walk away from ever needing to prove yourself again. This process is not about surviving. It's about freedom. Because without self-trust, we're never really free.

You already have everything you need to be successful. Now is about slowing down and doing the work to believe in yourself more. Self-trust is a gift you give yourself, but everyone else in your life benefits from it as well. It's okay to have your own back.

A bird sitting on a tree is never afraid of the branch breaking, because its trust is not on the branch but on its own wings.

–Unknown

CHAPTER FOUR
SUMMARY

- We always lose trust in ourselves when we're more concerned about losing others.

- If you ever need to choose between building trust with yourself or with someone else, always choose yourself.

- Self-trust is a clear and unwavering commitment to having your own back.

- The relationship you have with yourself often mirrors your relationships with others.

- Ten Actions That Will Help You Build Self-Trust:
  1. Honor Who You Are
  2. Act Like You Belong
  3. Grow Your Professional Competence
  4. Speak Up
  5. Take Ownership of Your Feelings
  6. Go on an "Advice Detox"
  7. Practice Forgiveness
  8. Believe in Something Bigger Than Yourself
  9. Get Yourself an Army
  10. Take Action

- You learn to trust yourself by taking action, not sitting on the sidelines talking about it.

CHAPTER FIVE

BUILDING TRUST WITH OTHERS

First step in leading:
Get the environment right!
Trust is what matters.

YOUR ROAD TO YES!

"Excuse me. Would you please raise your hand if you're flying to Indianapolis, Indiana?"

I heard those words as I sat at the gate in Denver International Airport on July 29, 2019. Everyone around the gate slowly stopped what they were doing, looked up with curiosity, and started to raise their hands.

"Hello, everyone. My name is Captain Dave Tuck, and I'll be flying your plane today. I like to know who is on my team, so I wanted to come out here and see you." The United Airlines pilot explained how he had served in the military, and he knows how important it is that everyone is on the same page. He briefed us on the flight time, the weather, and how we might be five minutes late, informing us that we had enough fuel to get to Antarctica if we needed to. He ended by saying, "I just have one rule today: Be kind to each other. Our flight attendants are on board. The plane is clean for you, and I look forward to a good trip. I'll see you in Indianapolis."

Captain Dave Tuck received roaring applause in the terminal. In a matter of a minute, he was able to communicate in a way that connected with others and made them feel like they could trust him. Many pilots communicate with their passengers, but not many of them connect the way Dave Tuck did. What did he do differently than so many others?

Dave used his presence to create an environment of trust where we all unconsciously said, "Yes!" He created trust by being fully transparent about his expectations. Did he take us with him along the journey? Yes. He was tactful and even used humor to deliver his message. Did he make the message and environment safe? Yes. And by the end, he made us feel like we were all in this together. Did we feel less alone? Yes. Those three factors are the foundation for earning and keeping trust in every relationship. Messages and relationships built on yes will always lead you to higher levels of trust.

Let's explore each trust factor and how you can apply them in how you show up every day.

JUSTIN PATTON

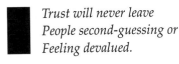

Trust will never leave
People second-guessing or
Feeling devalued.

COMMUNICATE WITH TRANSPARENCY

In 2019 I boarded a Delta Airlines flight headed to Detroit. The man in front of me put his bags in the overhead compartment. He then turned around and walked off the plane. I fly every month, so I knew that wasn't normal. A flight attendant would tackle most people if they tried to exit the plane without explanation. I got situated in my seat and jerked my head left and right to see if anyone else had seen the same thing. Everyone else was minding their own business and didn't seem to have a care in the world. I was thinking, "Am I being punked? Is this an episode of *What Would You Do?*"

I could feel my anxiety increasing as it was almost time to close the main cabin door. I started thinking the worst and said to myself, "I'm going to regret not saying anything if something ends up happening on this plane." I tried to build up my confidence to say something, but I didn't want to be the reason we were delayed. I then remembered the line they always broadcast in the airport: "If you see something, say something." I was like, "Oh hell no. We are not going down on my watch!" I got up and walked to the front of the plane. I said to the flight attendant, "Listen. I'm sure this is nothing, but a man put his bags up and then walked off the plane, and I haven't seen him return." She explained the man was an off-duty pilot, and he would be flying in the cockpit with the other pilots. He had gone to grab something to eat since he wouldn't have time on his layover.

I felt a little silly, but I was also proud of myself for saying something. I walked back to my seat and realized that all the anxiety I felt had left my body. This situation taught me about the power of transparency. Transparency creates clarity in our lives, and clarity always brings us more peace. I sat down, put in my headphones, and enjoyed the rest of the trip.

Transparency is the ability to communicate the what and the why. It does not require us to overwhelm people with every detail of our feelings, decision-making, or beliefs, but transparency does require us to share enough context so we're able to take people with us on the journey.

If truth makes our perspective known, then transparency is what makes it clear. When people don't have all the information behind why our truth is our truth, we send them on an emotional rollercoaster. They are often left to second-guess why we feel the way we do, why we made our decisions, and what this means for themselves or the relationship. Trust never leaves people second-guessing.

TRUST NEVER LEAVES PEOPLE SECOND-GUESSING.

I've often heard other speakers and leaders talk about the importance of setting boundaries, and then they ultimately say that classic line, "No is a complete sentence." I cringe a little every time I hear it. It's a great sound bite and often gets people to shake their heads in agreement. I understand. A sense of personal power comes when you imagine standing in your "NO"—especially when you've gone so long without standing up for yourself. However, responding with a singular "no" is only appropriate when you don't care about maintaining a relationship with the other person. No is a perfectly acceptable response, but it's not the complete sentence.

It's just as important to be transparent about why the answer is a no. Transparency provides context and clarity for others. They don't have to agree, accept, or appreciate the reasoning, but we provide it because that helps create mutual understanding and trust in the relationship.

Providing transparency to people doesn't require us to give away our power or make excuses for our position. If anything, it helps our position be known. It gives people the space to understand, ask questions, and share their perspectives. That should be the goal of any relationship focused on building trust.

I always think about how often parents tell their kids no, and when their child asks, "But why?" they respond with, "Because I said so!"

NO IS A PERFECTLY ACCEPTABLE RESPONSE, BUT IT'S NOT THE COMPLETE SENTENCE.

How would we feel if we asked our boss for a raise or additional resources and they said no, and when we asked why they responded with, "Because I said so." This lack of candor would make any of us feel dismissed and devalued. No is a perfectly acceptable response, but it's not the complete sentence. We would want to understand why the answer is a no so that we could make an informed decision about our next steps. Everyone deserves the respect of transparency.

I always laugh when I get a text message from a friend, and they ask, "Can you do me a favor?" I usually respond with something witty like, "I did you a favor when we became friends." As I laugh, I'm sitting there thinking, tell me what you want done, and I'll tell you if I can do it. How are they going to ask me to do something without any transparency behind the request? I know my friends, and I'm not agreeing to anything before I know the context. Transparency allows us to make more informed decisions, and it allows others to know why we make decisions.

Abby Ross Hopper, the President and CEO of the Solar Energy Industries Association (SEIA), artfully demonstrated the power of transparency during the COVID-19 pandemic. In April 2020, Abby brought her entire staff together because she wanted to keep them in the loop over what she was observing in the business and talk about contingencies they might have to make as a business to continue serving their members. She informed them they might have to make tough decisions, but she never wanted them to be in the dark. Therefore, she set up weekly all-staff meetings where she could share the state of the business, provide transparency on decisions, answer employees' questions, and make sure they felt informed. Ultimately, SEIA had to lay off seven employees, temporarily reduce all staff pay by 10 percent, and slash executive pay by 25 percent. Additionally, they temporarily stopped the 401K match during the height of the pandemic. None of the decisions came out of the blue for the staff. Not every employee agreed with the decisions, but they respected how the executive team made them. There was no hidden agenda or some grand reveal. Abby loved her staff enough to treat them respectfully and give them transparent information. When I followed up with the organization at the end of 2021, I asked the Chief Business Officer what impact they had seen from Abby's level of transparency. Mike told me, "The transparency Abby demonstrated helped her create stronger trust with the entire staff that is still present today." Abby now holds a monthly all-staff meeting, and people ask more direct questions. Her transparency has given them the space to do the same, and the trust she's created has increased the level of candor in the entire organization.

Let's explore six specific ways to foster transparency in your relationships and throughout the organization.

SIX WAYS LEADERS CAN FOSTER TRANSPARENCY

- Value Candor
- Share What's Below the Water Line
- Set Clear Expectations
- Ask for Feedback
- Own Your Mistakes
- Recognize the Brave

VALUE CANDOR

Candor is your ability to be honest about your perspective. And I've known many honest people who don't tell the truth. In uncomfortable moments, they bury their head in the sand and don't share what they feel and believe. They sometimes think they can bottle up the emotions and just move on. The reality is that they often just get resentful, and it's hard to come back from that feeling.

When you value candor, you love people enough to tell them your truth. You also accept that your truth isn't the only truth, and you provide them the space to open up, too. If the other person in your relationship doesn't value candor and gets upset when you try to share your thoughts and feelings, you are in the wrong relationship. You'll never be able to move a relationship forward with trust if you can't be candid with each other without feeling shamed and belittled.

Candor challenges leaders to avoid the trap of surrounding themselves with people who always believe the same and who just validate each other's perspectives. This mentality sabotages any diversity of thought and promotes groupthink in an organization.

To value candor, we must appreciate that everyone comes into the relationship with a different truth. Truth is not fact. Truth is a matter of perspective. We base our perspective on our values, past experiences, the people we surround ourselves with, and the information we choose to consume. These filters become the limits to how we see the world. Our truth is just a byproduct of these filters. It's not until we can see beyond ourselves and our current truth, and explore someone else's truth, that we open ourselves up to a new way of seeing.

I find that we value candor more when we genuinely believe in the power of collaboration. Collaboration means that this is not a relationship where someone wins, and someone loses. We are in this together, and our job is to make this a win-win for everyone involved. We can only do that by telling each other the truth and figuring out how to move forward in a way that works for everyone. This mindset promotes people being transparent with each other and doing so in a timely manner.

I have a friend whose manager came to him and highlighted some concerns about his performance a few months back. My friend was open to receiving the feedback and committed to making any necessary changes. However, he expressed that he felt a little blindsided by his manager. Most of the issues his manager raised came down to miscommunication. There was a clear lack of transparency on expectations and the feelings coming up with his performance. He wished his manager would have valued the relationship enough to say something sooner.

When we don't say what we need to say in relationships, we often replace candor with resentment, and everyone loses. If we want to be a leader in any relationship in our lives, then we must value candor. Candor always opens the door for transparency, and transparency is a key factor in building trust.

YOUR ROAD TO YES!

SHARE WHAT'S BELOW THE WATER LINE

Transparency requires you to explain what's below the water line. Below the water is all the stuff that isn't visible on the surface, but it's influencing the conversation. In that vulnerable space, we can discuss our emotions, our reasoning for why we made the decision, the missing pieces of information that someone doesn't have insight into, or the stories we've possibly created.

TRANSPARENCY REQUIRES YOU TO EXPLAIN WHAT'S BELOW THE WATER LINE.

In my earlier story on the Delta flight, what was visible was that a guy had put his luggage up and walked off the plane. That's the information that was on the surface. However, the transparency provided by the flight attendant about who the man was and what he was doing put me at ease. Those were the missing pieces of information under the water line that I would've never known had she not taken the time to explain them to me.

There are three specific phrases that, if you use them, will help you communicate with more transparency and help you get below the water line:

- I feel...
- I believe...
- The reason I/we...

I FEEL opens the door for people to share their emotions. I close my eyes a little longer than I should every time I hear someone say, "Feelings aren't facts" or "Leave emotions out of it." I find those comments ludicrous. Emotions drive everything purposeful and meaningful in our lives. There is so much research on the importance and impact of emotional intelligence on relationships and business. Our goal is not to get rid of emotion. Emotional intelligence is learning how to use emotions to build trust and move the conversation and relationship forward. You can't do that when you're not talking about your feelings. In the book *Difficult Conversations*, the authors highlight that one of the reasons most difficult conversations never get resolved is because we try to "leave emotion out of it." As a result, we never feel heard or get to the core issue.

EMOTIONAL INTELLIGENCE IS LEARNING HOW TO USE EMOTIONS TO BUILD TRUST AND MOVE THE CONVERSATION AND RELATIONSHIP FORWARD.

Letting someone know that you feel overwhelmed, excited, alone, helpless, or confused creates the potential for the conversation to go deeper. Emotions humanize and connect us. We owe it to ourselves to share what we're feeling and how those feelings drive our thoughts and actions. The more comfortable leaders get at expressing emotions, and why they're feeling those emotions, the more emotionally intelligent our organizational cultures become. Everyone wins when that happens!

I BELIEVE allows you to contribute your perspective to a conversation, so people know where you stand. Organizations hire you for your experience and skills. Part of the value you bring is the perspective you've learned along the way. This doesn't mean you have to speak up in every conversation, but you should speak up when your perspective would help move the conversation forward. Explain what you believe and why you believe what you do. You are paid to have a point of view.

THE REASON I/WE is the catalyst for sharing the why behind our decisions. So often, we only share the outcome with people: We are going to have layoffs. You are going to get a raise. I'd like for you to take on this stretch project. Our speed of service metric is now five seconds lower than before. The problem with only sharing the outcome is that it offers no insight into why and then people are left to make up the reason independently. This can be easily remedied when we say something like, "The reason we decided to shorten our speed of service time is that over 60 percent of the company is already hitting that metric; the new technology we're implementing will allow us to get orders out even faster; our competitors are already using this metric; and it's our way of pushing ourselves to continue to make a better customer experience." Not everyone will agree or like the explanation, but they will understand what informed the decision.

I once coached a Director of Operations who told me that morale from the people under him was worse than he'd ever seen before. He explained that he could usually inspire and pick people back up, but it had become more challenging than ever. When I asked what he believed was causing the moral issues, he stated a lot of it stemmed from decisions made by the executive leadership team and how they'd made so many decisions without communicating the why behind them. For example, they'd made it harder for their general managers to achieve their bonuses. The general managers didn't know if this policy was just temporary or permanent or what information had informed this decision. He also shared that there was a maximum cap on what they could hire someone at, but that the organization mandated general managers bring in team members at less money than the maximum, which made it harder to attract talent. He shared that many of the emails from the leadership team felt like reprimands, that you either do things a certain way or you'll be let go. He expressed that some managers worked fourteen hours a day and didn't feel seen or valued. He felt there was a huge transparency gap in the organization, and it was only causing frustration and people to leave.

Here's the deal: not everyone will like or appreciate your explanation of your decisions. You don't have to own that for them. Your goal as a leader is to communicate decisions as transparently as possible. It is not to convince everyone to buy into them. Our ability to understand the why behind our decisions is the initial first step in bringing people along the journey with us.

SET CLEAR EXPECTATIONS

I have a friend who recently started a new job. She called me up one day, gushing about her new manager. She said as soon as she began her role, the manager set up a meeting to get to know each other, discuss their work styles, and how they could best communicate. She highlighted that no other manager had ever done this in her career.

Unrelated, I once facilitated a DISC communication workshop when someone stopped in the middle of the debrief and yelled, "Every married couple should have to go through this together!" We all laughed and nodded our heads in agreement.

Both examples highlight the value and importance of setting clear expectations. In a world where it feels like we're always rushing around and busy-being-busy, taking the time to be transparent about who we are and what we need from each other is a game-changer. When leaders fail to set clear expectations, they set up everyone for failure—including themselves. Excellent performance and trust-building are a result of clear expectations.

I believe there are two types of expectations all great leaders are transparent about: performance expectations and behavior expectations.

Performance expectations identify *what* you should focus on to achieve success. Great managers communicate a vision for the result, not the detailed process for how someone achieves that result. The best managers allow space for team members to bring their unique skills, creativity, and ideas to complete tasks. The only time managers should dictate the process is when associates must follow specific safety, consistency, or measurability steps.

Behavioral expectations identify *how* you should show up in the process of driving results. These expectations signal the behavior and actions that are okay and not okay. I've coached many "high performers" who were excellent at meeting performance expectations but not nearly as mindful of the behaviors they demonstrated to get those results.

Setting clear expectations is not a one-time event where you are transparent about your needs and never talk about them again. It's an ongoing practice of checking in, recognizing others when they do things well, encouraging others to ask clarifying questions, and leaning into uncomfortable conversations when we need to realign. This is how we create transparency that builds trust.

YOUR ROAD TO YES!

ASK FOR FEEDBACK

Asking someone for feedback is a great way to invite transparency in a way that might not have happened otherwise. I once had a weekly one-on-one meeting with my assistant, and I asked her, "What would you be doing differently if this business was yours?" She thought for a moment and then told me there was an opportunity to automate more processes to make our jobs easier and get stuff out to our clients more quickly. She was right! We've now implemented more automated processes because of her feedback.

My assistant and I have a great relationship, and I believe she feels safe coming to talk to me or give me feedback. However, maybe in the busyness of everything else, she wouldn't have given me that feedback had I not asked. Asking an open-ended question and being genuinely open to whatever answer the other person says is a safe way to invite transparency and trust in your relationships.

OWN YOUR MISTAKES

So, you mess up. It sucks. You're nervous. You're fretting about the course of action and the consequences. Those are all natural feelings. However, leaders who want to role-model transparency and accountability commit to one fundamental next step: own it, learn from it, and move on.

When I transitioned from being a high school English teacher to teaching adults in corporate America, I joined UniCare. I knew nothing about health insurance, but I was committed to learning. One day I sent an email out to a large number of agents. One of them replied and chastised me for making everyone's email visible and told me I violated the Health Insurance Portability and Accountability Act of 1996 (HIPAA), which protected sensitive patient health information from being disclosed without the patient's consent. I sat there at my desk, my heart started racing, and all I could think about was, "The HIPAA police are coming for me." I'm confident enough to tell you that I cannot make it in jail, and I have no intentions of going. I immediately went to my boss and told him what I had done. He chuckled and reassured me it had nothing to do with HIPAA and that the healthcare police weren't coming for me. He then thanked me for sharing the information with him, and we had a long conversation about how to approach the situation differently the next time. The transparency we demonstrated that day only added to our trust for each other.

RECOGNIZE THE BRAVE

Transparency can feel risky for some, depending on their level of confidence, role, and safety in the organization. Workplaces that want to encourage transparent communication need to create intentional opportunities to recognize the brave, both publicly and privately. This reinforces the behavior of the person who spoke up and sends a message that this behavior is expected and rewarded. Remember: what gets rewarded is what gets reinforced. Thank people who speak up and share a different perspective in a healthy way. Have a high-five party for individuals who pushed the group to think differently and added value to the business. Build up people who make an isolated mess-up and have the courage to own their mistakes quickly to mitigate problems. You cannot have transparency without vulnerability. Vulnerability takes courage, so recognize the brave in your organization.

WHAT GETS REWARDED IS WHAT GETS REINFORCED.

YES! TO TRANSPARENCY

Transparency is a foundational factor in our ability to build trust with others. It challenges you to ask yourself, "Do I take people with me along the journey?" Transparency is how you gain buy-in. When we can answer "YES!" and when others believe us, we earn and keep others' trust.

- Which relationships in your life would benefit from more transparency?
- What do those individuals need to know or hear from you right now?
- What's stopping you from communicating that message?

Your presence should always be one where people know where you stand, come to you because of your honesty, and feel invited to do the same.

SUMMARY

- Transparency does require us to share enough context so we're able to take people with us on the journey.

- Trust never leaves people second-guessing.

- No is a perfectly acceptable response, but it's not the complete sentence.

- Six Ways Leaders Can Foster Transparency:
  1. Value Candor
  2. Share What's Below the Water Line
  3. Set Clear Expectations
  4. Ask for Feedback
  5. Own Your Mistakes
  6. Recognize the Brave

- Three specific phrases that will help you communicate with more transparency and get below the water line:
  1. I feel…
  2. I believe…
  3. The reason I/we…

- Emotional intelligence is learning how to use emotions to build trust and move the conversation and relationship forward.

- Two types of expectations all great leaders are transparent about regularly:
  1. Performance Expectations
  2. Behavior Expectations

- What gets rewarded is what gets reinforced.

- Transparency requires you to be able to answer "YES!" to the following question:
  Do I take people with me along the journey?

JUSTIN PATTON

 *You cannot have trust
where there is fear and judgment.
Safety is the key.*

COMMUNICATE WITH TACT

My sister and I have a great relationship. However, like most siblings, we'll sometimes joke and poke fun at each other. Showing empathy is a skill I've worked on over the years, but sometimes I'll show empathy in a joking way with my sister because it makes us laugh. However, I now know I need to be more mindful when choosing those moments.

My sister had just come home from the gym, and she was complaining about how bad her toes hurt from breaking in new tennis shoes. I went to the first aid kit and got her some Band-Aids to wrap her toe. As I handed them to her, I tilted my head to the side and sarcastically said, "Wow, sis. It sounds and looks like you've had a really rough morning."

Well, she wasn't having it. Her pain took over, and she snapped back, "See, this is why you're single!"

She's lucky I teach emotional intelligence because it took everything I had not to snap back, pull something out of her baggage, and use it against her. I didn't want to be that person, however. I had already been that person enough in my past. I closed my eyes, gave myself about three seconds not to go all NeNe Leakes from *Real Housewives of Atlanta* on her, and then I calmly said, "Wow, sis. I'm surprised you'd take something vulnerable about me and use it against me."

Because I communicated calmly, lowered my tone, and removed judgment from my response, she was able to look at how she was responding. As a result, she started to match my energy. We had a productive conversation about why that comment triggered me and why she lashed out the way she did, and a short time later, we were laughing with each other. Me sharing my truth, being transparent about why it bothered me, and maintaining my ability to be tactful resulted in a conversation that kept our trust entact. Had I been transparent but lacked tact, she would have stormed off or just become agreeable and silent. Either way, the relationship would have suffered at that moment.

Tact is the ability to manage your intensity. More importantly, tact is the ultimate display of care in a relationship. It's your demonstration that the relationship means enough to keep yourself in check and not say something you'll regret later. Relationships can't survive someone trying to constantly apologize their way through them.

TACT IS THE ULTIMATE DISPLAY OF CARE IN A RELATIONSHIP.

THE ROLE OF PSYCHOLOGICAL SAFETY

I've always believed that organizations thrive or die based on middle management, and that's because those leaders have the most impact on an employee's day-to-day experience. Executive leaders create the vision for the culture, but managers decide whether to bring that vision to life or not based on the energy they show up with every day and the behaviors they reward. Great management makes all the difference in every organization and employee's life.

In 2012, Google set out to understand what factors created high-performing teams. They coined this research "Project Aristotle." The project took over two years, and the research team studied over 180 teams inside Google. In 2014 when the project leads shared their findings inside the company, they had determined that psychological safety—more than anything else—led to high-performing teams. Since then, research has consistently reinforced the necessity and benefit of psychological safety on workplace performance and culture.

All leaders are in the safety business, and each leader has a pivotal responsibility of cultivating psychological safety in the workplace. When that happens, they signal that authenticity, candor, and risk-taking are not just welcome but expected here.

PSYCHOLOGICAL SAFETY—MORE THAN ANYTHING ELSE—LED TO HIGH-PERFORMING TEAMS.

Years ago, I had the chance to interview the former CEO of Yum! Brands and Taco Bell, Greg Creed. He said to me, "If you ever have to give up who you are for a job, then you're in the wrong job." Greg knew that authenticity and vulnerability were a competitive advantage for an organization and that customers ultimately reaped the benefits. This insight also taught me that sometimes we spend so much energy waiting for an organization to create psychological safety with us when the right next step might be to create it for ourselves—even if that means leaving.

Psychological safety allows you the freedom to show up as exactly who you are, warts and all, and still feel valued. That doesn't mean you're not working on yourself, excusing bad behavior, or eliminating the blind spots that might hold you back. It simply means your presence and ideas are already good enough, and you're worthy of being heard. Organizations start to create an inclusive environment where all people feel their authentic self is valued when they arrive. That's psychological safety in action!

Many of us worked for a manager who led out of fear and defaulted to an authoritative leadership style. That manager might have scored results, but they often never scored our trust and loyalty. In their 2021 article *Psychological Safety and the Critical Role of Leadership Development*, McKinsey & Company stated that "authoritative-leadership behaviors are detrimental to psychological safety." Fear can incite immediate action, but it's not a sustainable model for building high-performing teams and a culture of belonging. A lack of psychological safety causes our body to release cortisol which is the stress hormone in our bodies. Cortisol catapults us into a survival mode; therefore, we question intentions and make decisions in our best interests to survive the short-term moment. You cannot build trust when your focus is on survival. Psychological safety requires leaders to focus on more collaborative behaviors that make people feel part of a team.

Psychological safety allows us to create a culture of belonging. The "2020 Global Human Capital Trends" report identified belonging as one of the most important human capital issues. Their research found that 93 percent agreed that a sense of belonging drives organizational performance, but only 13 percent said they were ready to address the trend.

Creating a workplace of psychological safety isn't necessarily easy. Those workplace environments are rare, according to the *Harvard Business Review* article "4 Steps to Boost Psychological Safety at Your Workplace." Authors Amy Edmondson and Per Hugander say the reason is simple: "It's natural for people to hold back ideas, be reluctant to ask questions, and shy away from disagreeing with their boss...To reverse it takes focus and effort; it's a process of helping people develop new beliefs and behaviors, and none of it is easy or natural."

Below are ten actions all leaders can take to create psychological safety on a team:

1. Check-in regularly
2. Encourage idea sharing
3. Invite and give feedback
4. Squash judgment
5. Admit mistakes
6. Ask questions
7. Show empathy
8. Champion diversity
9. Assign team collaborations
10. Reward candor

Companies focused on psychological safety must take a holistic approach to upgrade the employee experience and retain staff. It's no longer enough only to care what happens to them during their regular work hours. Psychological safety requires managers to invest in their team members' whole lives and prioritize mental and emotional wellness. Managers can't emotionally bankrupt their staff and then expect them to show up cheerful and ready to give it their all. Their "all" was depleted months ago, and we often fail

> MANAGERS CAN'T EMOTIONALLY BANKRUPT THEIR STAFF AND THEN EXPECT THEM TO SHOW UP CHEERFUL AND READY TO GIVE IT THEIR ALL.

to notice. We must check in regularly, listen with the intent to understand, share practical ideas on how to recharge, and discuss how we move forward together. Only with that level of candor and authenticity can we create a space that works for everyone!

One of your greatest accomplishments is being in a relationship where you feel safe. It doesn't just happen, though. It takes work, vulnerable communication, and the commitment to put the relationship above yourself. You cannot have trust without safety. Trust is the outcome of safety in a relationship, and we all perform and compete better when we feel safe.

I want to be clear about something. I'm not saying you should never raise your voice. In fact, that's sometimes the only way for someone to understand the seriousness of a situation. You already know what I mean if you are a parent. However, it should not be your go-to or consistent response. If so, you just say a lot of nothing, creating a dynamic of phycological fear in the relationship. Your lack of tact then becomes a form of manipulation to bully people into submission. It will not serve you well in the long term.

I've coached many leaders who lead their teams out of fear. It is dangerous to put insecure people into positions of leadership. You'll know they are insecure when they dominate every conversation, only listen to be right, and intimidate others out of their best thinking. Their lack of tact when communicating will make them feel in charge and in control, but their response is rooted in insecurity. The longer they are allowed to be in a position of power, the more miserable it becomes for everyone else around them. Their leadership is toxic. They destroy trust. They erode the very fabric of the culture created, and people will ultimately jump ship because the murky water below feels safer than the people they know on board.

Every leader has the critical responsibility of creating an environment where physical and emotional safety are present. Those are fundamental to communicating with tact. Let's explore seven ways leaders can communicate with tact in the workplace and at home:

SEVEN WAYS LEADERS CAN COMMUNICATE WITH TACT

- Listen to Understand
- Detach from the Outcome
- Pause Before Responding
- Wear Concrete Boots
- Name Your Emotions
- Honor Who You Are At Your Best
- Practice Gentleness

LISTEN TO UNDERSTAND

Listening is the first fundamental step if we want to understand someone else's truth. "Truth" is a dangerous word when we confuse it with "fact." We often believe our truth is the absolute truth, and we think other people are crazy if they don't agree or understand our point of view. This mentality holds us back in every relationship because of one main reason. We attach our knowledge to our sense of identity and become defensive when someone has a different perspective. Our ego fools us into believing we must defend ourselves in every conversation. We stop listening to understand. As a result, we self-designate ourselves as president of the "truth squad" and round up everyone else for trial. We then communicate with judgment, pettiness, and shaming. You cannot have trust where there is judgment.

YOU CANNOT HAVE TRUST WHERE THERE IS JUDGMENT.

In my first book, *Bold New You*, I write that "You can listen to be right or listen to understand, but you cannot do both. Each of those requires a different intention and presence in the conversation. Leaders who do not listen or only listen to be right take more than your time and energy; they take your trust. Listening to understand requires intentionality and for you to listen deeper than just the words being said." Thich Nhat Hanh, Vietnamese Buddhist monk and peace activist, described deep listening as "the kind of listening that can relieve the suffering of the other person. You listen with one purpose: help him or her to empty his heart."

Listening is hard for all of us when we show up with a mindset that we must prove, justify, or defend ourselves. This posturing often causes us to interrupt and dismiss what others have to say. We then only listen for the parts of the conversations we can use to demonstrate why our perspective is right. There is no learning in this type of dialogue. There is only defensiveness. Deep listening requires you to be fully present for the people in front of you. It's about listening so intuitively that you can understand the emotion underneath what they are saying. It's asking yourself, "I wonder why they believe what they do?" and then following up with questions from a place of genuine curiosity. It's acknowledging their point of view, so they feel seen and heard. Deep listening is how we connect, and that doesn't require you to agree with everyone in the process.

DETACH FROM THE OUTCOME

INTENSITY INTIMIDATES PEOPLE OUT OF THEIR BEST THINKING.

Tact tends to fly out the window when we feel we must defend ourselves or persuade others. We get so attached to the outcome we want that our intensity often gets the best of us. I once had the chance to interview Melissa Lora, the former President of Taco Bell International. We had a great discussion on the role intensity plays in trust. She said, "Leaders become so attached to the outcome they desire that they do not sit back and create space in meetings to activate other's brilliance. Their energy heats up the room, and everyone can feel it. Intensity intimidates people out of their best thinking. It can erode influence and trust. Because they are so focused on 'the pitch' that they are trying to make, they forget who is on their team and how collectively they may innovate to create a better outcome. As a result, everyone loses."

Leaders communicate better and cultivate trust with others when they can share their truth and then detach from the outcome.

Detachment does not mean you do not come into the conversation with a clear perspective. It means you are willing to take a step back from your truth, listen to others, and co-create a conversation and solution together. It positions you as a team player who doesn't always have to get their way or shoot the game-winning shot at the end of every game. Detaching allows you to stay tactful and build trust.

PAUSE BEFORE RESPONDING

Our parents teach us as kids to always look both ways before we cross the street. We go near the edge of the curb, pause, look left, right, left, and then make a run for it. They teach this to protect us and make sure there's no accident. Wouldn't that concept be just as helpful if we carried it forward into how we communicate as adults?

I'm sure we all had moments in the middle of a conversation when we should have paused and looked at the options available before responding. However, emotion takes over, and we take off running, and that's when accidents happen. We all remember Will Smith getting out of his chair during the 2022 Oscars, walking up on stage, and slapping Chris Rock for making a joke aimed at Jada Pinkett Smith. Smith's behavior was inappropriate, and everyone deserved better at that moment. The inability to pause led Smith to act in ways that didn't create safety.

The pause is the differentiator. It's the space where we choose to respond with emotional intelligence and honor the best of who we are or to react out of ego. Sometimes ego can make us feel good in the moment. We want to be right. We want to get the last word. It's easier to criticize and shame others than to breathe and ask ourselves, "What choice would I make if I was focused on building trust?" However, the latter option better serves us and our relationships. It also brings more peace, and we could also use a little more of that in our lives.

Practicing the pause isn't easy. In a culture consumed by noise, pauses challenge us to become more comfortable with stillness. Only then can we look before we leap and make more informed choices.

WEAR CONCRETE BOOTS

This technique is for all the passionate people out there whose intensity can sometimes get the best of them. At times, I can get so into a conversation that I jump in and cut people off, take up a lot of space with my gestures, and only listen to hear when I can insert my thoughts. That intensity can erode safety in a conversation. Therefore, I practice sitting back in my chair and pretending to wear concrete boots. The concrete boots require me to stay grounded, prevent me from dancing around in my chair, and focus my energy on where it should be: the other person.

NAME YOUR EMOTIONS

Years ago, some friends and I went to the Haunted House at Wavery Hills Sanatorium in Louisville, KY. I found most of it funny until we got into a large empty room. I could see a guy hiding in the left corner. I yelled to the group to watch it because he was going to jump out. As soon as I got into the middle of the room, he released a rope he was holding. A giant stuffed tarantula with long dangling legs fell right on top of my head. I hate spiders! In fact, the only movie I've screamed out loud at is *Arachnophobia*. The moment those dangly hairy legs hit my head, I fell straight on the ground, screamed four octaves higher, and used my feet to kick the monster away. I swear I would have won America's Funniest Home Videos had it been recorded.

So when my best friend asked me later in life if I wanted to hold Rosie the Tarantula at the Butterfly Pavilion in Westminster, Colorado, I immediately exclaimed, "Oh, hell no!" Rosie is the Pavilion's ambassador, and kids go through there all day holding her and learning the important role spiders play in our ecosystem. The only role they play in my life is out of sight, out of mind. I was baffled by why people would do such a thing. Then something in my mind said, "What if this is your chance to face your fears?" I leveraged my emotional intelligence training, where we teach people that you have to "name it to tame it." You name the emotions you feel once you're emotionally hijacked. I told Chad, "Okay. I'm feeling scared, and like I might pee a little. I'm nervous because what if this spider decides that I'm the person she will take all of her frustration out on?" You can see I use humor to deal with uncomfortable situations sometimes. Naming the emotions did make it easier. I was still scared, but the fear wasn't paralyzing. It didn't prevent me from moving forward. I sat down in the chair, and the handler put Rosie on my hand. I gave it a few good seconds before letting them know that Rosie and I had our moment and she could leave now.

When you're feeling an overwhelming deluge of emotions, or you can tell your intensity is getting in the way of being tactful, a good action to take is simply to name your emotion(s). Classifying your feelings can dampen their charge. It allows you a chance to regain rational control and express what you feel, so you can make better choices on how to move forward.

HONOR WHO YOU ARE AT YOUR BEST

One morning I found myself being easily annoyed and critical of others. It all started when I got to the airport and had trouble finding a parking spot. I then got "randomly selected" to go through additional security screening. You know I questioned how random it was. I got situated in my seat on the plane, put my headphones in, and closed my eyes. I was shoulder-blocked by what had to be a few NFL linebackers as they made their way to their seats. I remember thinking I was about to go full-on Carrie Underwood with that Louisville Slugger bat she sang about.

I told myself to pull it together. My negative attitude impacted my morning and my ability to connect with others, and I don't want to be that type of person. I took a few deep breaths and prayed for some grace because I would need it that morning! I closed my eyes, listened to my gospel playlist, and reminded myself of the truth of who I am: confident, empathetic, and fully present.

We all get irritable. We all are human. It's okay. However, we must be aware that we are being a "Judgey Judy" and then decide if we want to show up differently. Negativity is easy. It gives us a permission slip to avoid looking at ourselves by being a victim and blaming everyone else for our negative attitude. Taking responsibility for our energy isn't always convenient or easy. It requires intentionality and the willingness to slow down and walk back into the truth of who we are when we are our best. The choice is always ours.

The first exercise I do with all my coaching clients is to have them identify a time in their life they showed up their best, personally or professionally. They describe that moment to me. I then ask, "What were the top three actions you demonstrated that allowed you to show up that way?" I often hear words like confident, empathetic, fully present, knowledgeable, prepared, kind, and fun. After some self-exploration, they learn that when they're showing up their best in all parts of their life, it's usually because they're living these three actions out consistently. This vision for who you are at your best will help you always speak with more tact, especially in difficult moments. Those moments are the most important ones. Can we stay true to who we are even when the world pushes and prods us? That's authentic leadership, and this vision will be the anchor you need to speak in a way that honors both you and the relationships in your life.

PRACTICE GENTLENESS

I read a line from Gandhi that disrupted and challenged my thinking. He said, "In a gentle way, you can shake the world." It got me thinking about what gentleness is and the impact it has on how our ability to lead, love, and communicate.

My favorite definition of gentleness is "strength under control." It's acknowledging that you have the power to yield force in every situation, but you choose to manage the intensity. Gentleness is a sign of high emotional intelligence in all leaders because instead of overreacting, they choose to remain in control of what they're thinking and feeling. That is not weakness. That is exactly the type of strength we need out of our leaders.

I went horseback riding in the countryside of Berlin on September 12, 2019. Inge, the farm owner, gave us instructions about putting on the bridle properly. She said, "Be gentle. Take your time. These horses do everything for us." What a great lesson on working with horses and even leading people. Our employees do everything for us! They make our jobs easier, allow us to accomplish more, and help us build a brand we are proud of. We leaders can hold the reins too tightly and spend so much energy controlling the journey that we make everyone miserable in the process. Or, we can hold the reins gently, pull back when we need to set boundaries, and be both direct and kind in the directions we give. The latter always creates a more enjoyable experience for everyone. Gentle does not mean we are weak. Gentle means we are patient and have a clear purpose. The best leaders know how to get results while still being gentle.

Jacinda Ardern, the fortieth prime minister of New Zealand, said, "One of the criticisms I've faced over the years is that I'm not aggressive enough or assertive enough, or maybe somehow, because I'm empathetic, it means I'm weak. I totally rebel against that. I refuse to believe that you cannot be both compassionate and strong."

Anger is easy. It doesn't require inner strength, self-control, or the ability to consider the long-term consequences. Anger is only fixated on winning the short-term moment, and the intensity is usually so strong that people become more fixated on the anger versus the message. You lose when that happens. When you refuse to allow someone's anger to dictate your actions or what you believe about yourself, you take their control away. You teach them that you deserve better and that they'll treat you better, or you'll leave.

In a world where anger is easy, gentleness is the most rebellious act. It's rebellious because it's the exact opposite of how people think you will respond—and therefore, it sticks!

I think of gentleness as responding with the least amount of force necessary to create change. Examples of how gentleness disrupted society were when Rosa Parks took a seat in the front of the bus, Colin Kaepernick took a knee during the National Anthem at a football game, and Hawaiian activists blocked the road to the summit of Mauna Kea on the Big Island of Hawaii. These

IN A WORLD WHERE ANGER IS EASY, GENTLENESS IS THE MOST REBELLIOUS ACT.

quiet acts of sitting on a bus seat, kneeling, and standing in front of an entrance sent a shockwave through society, garnered more attention for their causes, and ignited much-needed conversations. Gandhi was right. Gentleness shook things up!

Gentleness is a moment-by-moment decision we make to move through life with compassion and strength. It is not remaining silent on the things that are important to us or acquiescing to others' expectations. It is responding in the quietest way possible but still challenging people to look at themselves in the mirror.

Pastor Rick Warren once spoke on the strength of gentleness. Towards the end of his sermon, he mentioned three specific ways we can all practice gentleness: "1) When someone serves me, be understanding, not demanding; 2) When someone disagrees with me, be tender without surrender; and 3) When someone disappoints me, be gentle, not judgmental."

I was so invested in the topic of gentleness that I hired the research firm at the University of Northern Colorado to see if there was any correlation between leadership effectiveness and gentleness. The team launched a nationwide survey of 1,217 individuals. The results came back in January 2021, and they were unambiguous. Gentleness is a key component of good leadership in the workplace and is highly related to creating a trusting workplace culture with high outcomes.

Here are a few specific findings from the research:

- 74 percent perceive gentleness as a strength
- 74 percent agreed that the people they look up to are gentle in their approach
- 75 percent agreed that demonstrating gentleness makes them more effective
- 79 percent agreed that self-control is critical in one's ability to demonstrate gentleness
- 80 percent agree that civility is critical in one's ability to demonstrate gentleness

Gentleness is cultivated out of strength and demonstrated out of radical love. It is easy to lash out, pull back and disconnect, or allow our judgment to overtake our compassion. Trust is always sacrificed when that happens. We lead, love, and communicate better when we operate from a place of gentleness. It's not easy. We must make intentional choices to show up this way. Gentleness does not require us to back down or shy away. It requires us to take full responsibility for our presence and allow our candor to be balanced with self-control. For me, gentleness is a reminder of who I am when I am at my best. It is a reminder of the greatness I was born with. We all have access to it. We just have to believe in its power more than fear. I know that gentleness required more of my courage and strength than fear ever did.

We all make better choices when we allow gentleness to be our guide. What choice would you make if you were coming from a place of gentleness?

YES! TO TACT

Tact is how you create safety in a relationship, and safety always leads to higher levels of trust. The road to yes in every relationship must be traveled with safety. Your presence should always create security in the spaces you occupy. Without it, most people are reluctant to be transparent, and they definitely won't feel like they're part of a team. They will eventually take a different path.

- Does your intensity ever get the best of you?
- What would happen in your relationships if you could communicate without the intensity?
- What coping strategy can you try the next time you feel your intensity taking over?

Communicating with tact challenges you to manage your intensity so you can answer yes to the following question: "Do I create a safe space for people to open up?" Only through "YES!" can we lead effectively and earn and keep others' trust.

SUMMARY

- Tact is the ability to manage your intensity.
- Tact is the ultimate display of care in a relationship.
- It's psychological safety that allows us to create a culture of belonging.
- Ten actions leaders can take to create psychological safety on a team:
  1. Check-in regularly
  2. Encourage idea sharing
  3. Invite and give feedback
  4. Squash judgment
  5. Admit mistakes
  6. Ask questions
  7. Show empathy
  8. Champion diversity
  9. Assign team collaborations
  10. Reward candor
- Trust is the outcome of safety in a relationship.
- Seven ways leaders can communicate with tact:
  1. Listen to Understand
  2. Detach from the Final Outcome
  3. Pause Before Responding
  4. Sit Back and Wear Concrete Boots
  5. Name Your Emotions
  6. Honor Who You Are At Your Best
  7. Practice Gentleness
- Tact requires you to be able to answer "YES!" to the following question:
  Do I create a safe space for people to open up?

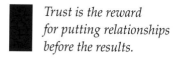

Trust is the reward
for putting relationships
before the results.

COMMUNICATE WITH TOGETHERNESS

I recently watched the Hulu show *Nine Perfect Strangers*. At one point, Nicole Kidman's character is standing on the edge of a cliff, and people think she will jump. A woman goes over to her, and Kidman yells, "I want you to step away!" The woman replies, "I'm not going to do that, but what I am going to do is hold your hand." The characters interlock fingers and stand there talking.

This emotional connection of togetherness is how trust feels. It's that moment when you want to push everyone away and handle everything on your own, but then someone reminds you that you don't have to make that choice.

Millions of people get up every day and feel like they're standing on the edge of a cliff in their relationships, jobs, health status, and finances. They want to move forward, but they don't know how. Here's the good news. You don't have to have the answers for these people. You just need to be willing to stand behind them, hold their hand, and remind them that they're not alone.

A key to building trust is focusing on "togetherness." Togetherness is your ability to make people feel like part of a team. I've coached married couples who feel alone, employees who go into an office every day and feel deserted by their manager until there's a problem, and kids too scared to talk to their parents because they're afraid they'll be shamed. They don't feel like they're part of a team.

TOGETHERNESS IS YOUR ABILITY TO MAKE PEOPLE FEEL LIKE PART OF A TEAM.

Did you ever see the *Titanic* movie with Leonardo DiCaprio and Kate Winslet? Well, spoiler alert! Kate's character, Rose, survives in the end because she floated on the door in the middle of the ocean until she was rescued. Rose never entertained the idea of Jack trying to get on the door with her. I'm convinced there was plenty of space on that door for both. Rose wasn't focused on being a team player in the critical moment that mattered. She was focused on her survival. We've all worked with a Rose before!

When we're in a relationship with someone more focused on themselves than what is best for the relationship, we often feel exhausted. Healthy relationships require you to be a team player! That means you show up consistently, communicate transparently, and do your part to make it a great experience for everyone involved. People build trust with each other when they're focused on building the relationship together. You can't do that when someone is more focused on being a solo artist.

TEAMWORK IS REALLY A FORM OF TRUST.

In Pat Summitt's book, *Reach for the Summit*, she shares twelve mindsets on succeeding at whatever you do. One of those mindsets is, "Put the team before yourself." She goes on to say, "Teamwork does not come naturally... Teamwork is not a matter of persuading yourself and your colleagues to set aside personal ambitions for the greater good. It's a matter of recognizing that your personal ambitions and the team's ambitions are one and the same. That's the incentive. Teamwork is really a form of trust."

When you focus on togetherness, you put the relationship's goals before your individual goals. That doesn't mean you don't take care of yourself. It does mean that you express your dreams and wants to the other person and include them in the process. Trust takes people along the journey. It doesn't leave people blind-sided or stranded. Putting the relationship before yourself requires you to make decisions that honor the relationship over your short-term satisfaction.

If you want to have a relationship built on togetherness, where teamwork is the foundation, you must have a mindset that supports that vision. Healthy relationships are built on "and," not "or." When we build relationships on "and," both people feel supported and believe they're stronger with the relationship than without it.

An example of this would be an employee driving results in the organization and their boss providing them with recognition and higher visibility in the company. Both people rely on each other to create results and look good. This type of relationship dynamic is a win-win for all parties involved.

Another example is a boss giving someone the feedback they need to grow and move forward in the organization and their career. Constructive feedback isn't always easy to hear, but the manager values the relationship enough to provide feedback so the other person can grow and continue the relationship. That's a win-win. Relationships built on "or" always feel limiting and restricting. Someone feels they constantly have to choose who will benefit from the decisions made. As a result, someone always feels left out. An example would be an employee not having a difficult conversation with someone because they don't want to deal with the emotional toll. That's more about their comfort than what's best for the relationship or the business.

I've always admired improv performers, and there's a lot we can learn from their craft. Successful improv requires people to be in relationships focused on "and." It requires you to build off each other's ideas, acknowledge each other's feelings, and commit to making the moment work together. Improvisers who build their relationships and conversations off of "or" are scene-stealers, putting their survival and success above everyone else's.

You cannot be successful at improv or in healthy relationships when you are focused on yourself and the goal of being the star. Trust is built when everyone is focused on each other's survival and success. We succeed together, and we fail together. Regardless, we have each other's back every step of the way. That's why togetherness makes people feel less alone in the world.

TRUST IS BUILT WHEN EVERYONE IS FOCUSED ON EACH OTHER'S SURVIVAL AND SUCCESS.

There will be times when every organization must make strategic decisions that are in the company's best interest versus the best interest of certain employees. That's because executives have a responsibility to ensure the company will be around in the future. It can feel that the company is more focused on "or" versus "and" – especially if those decisions impact you. However, a company's primary relationship is with its customers. Every company makes a daily commitment to their customers that their services will deliver what they said they would do—add value to their life and be around when they're needed again. The relationship with customers allows everyone else in the organization to have jobs, so executive leaders must always put that relationship first. That doesn't mean they don't care about you or don't want what's best for you and your family. It means that they must make decisions that look out for the future of all families, not just yours.

We live at a time when so many people feel disconnected. Leadership is about taking responsibility for your role in creating spaces focused on togetherness. Let's explore six ways leaders can create that sense of togetherness.

SIX WAYS LEADERS CREATE A SENSE OF TOGETHERNESS

- Demonstrate Consistency
- Put Empathy Before Information
- Commit to Availability
- Be a Team Player
- Spend Quality Time Together
- Create Personalized Touchpoints

DEMONSTRATE CONSISTENCY

Someone once told me, "If you're going to be anything in life, be consistent. At least then people know what to expect out of you." Consistency is what creates safety and trust in our relationships. When people don't know what version of you they're going to get on a certain day, they pull back, avoid honest conversations, and stand guard for the day and moment they can tell you what they need to tell you. It's emotionally exhausting, and your relationships cannot survive that environment long-term. You wouldn't continue to buy from a brand that was inconsistent in its products and commitments.

YOUR ROAD TO YES!

Why would you continue to invest in a person who demonstrates the same behavior?

Watch how someone consistently treats people they don't know, communicates in difficult moments, or celebrates others' success. Those moments can give you glimpses into who someone is, teach you about their character, and show how they will inevitably treat you. Most people will treat you well when they're trying to prove themselves. Watch how they treat those they're not trying to impress. Does that version of them put you at ease, make you proud of them, and encourage you to be around them more?

Inconsistency breeds fear and an environment where people walk on eggshells waiting to see which version of you they will get. Trust can't thrive under the weight of broken eggshells. Consistency in your actions is a cornerstone of togetherness. It's your commitment to others that they can trust in your presence. You will do what you say you're going to do. You will show up and live the values you say are important, and you will manage your energy so people know what they can expect from you.

CONSISTENCY IN YOUR ACTIONS IS A CORNERSTONE OF TOGETHERNESS.

PUT EMPATHY BEFORE INFORMATION

Great leaders, especially in emotionally charged situations, put empathy before information. They understand their value does not come in having all the answers. Their value comes in connecting, making people feel less alone in the world, and giving others the space to come up with their answers, leaving them feeling more empowered.

I was on social media one day when I received the following message:

"Hey, Justin! I was wondering if it would be okay to ask you a leadership question? I have a supervisor who doesn't really deserve the title; in fact, kind of abuses it… It's difficult working with her day-to-day; even though I try to help, it usually gets thrown back in my face…how would you handle this situation? Or what's your advice? She's been absent a lot lately…we are supposed to have Monday meetings, but she keeps canceling those too. When we do have them, it's about what she has to say, and if I say anything, it's either disregarded, not listened to, or she instantly goes on the defensive… when I try to help her, she throws it back in my face… Needless to say, not a positive working relationship…we have different personality types, and we started off on the wrong foot…I keep trying to get back on track, but I keep getting derailed by her behaviors."

This individual says she wants my advice in the message, but I believe what most people want initially is to be seen and validated for what they're feeling. She doesn't need me to jump in right away and impart my "wisdom." What she needs is for someone to say, "Wow. This sounds rough! It can feel emotionally exhausting to go to work every day and work with someone you want to have a good relationship with but don't feel is interested in doing the same with you."

Watch what happens when empathy is done well. If you get to the heart of what the person is feeling and experiencing, they'll usually nod or say, "Yes!" In the YES, you make people feel seen, heard, and valued. Empathy is the most effective and quickest way to build trust when communicating.

EMPATHY IS THE WILLINGNESS TO SEE BEYOND YOURSELF AND ACKNOWLEDGE WHAT SOMEONE IS FEELING, THINKING, AND CARRYING AROUND.

Empathy is the willingness to see beyond yourself and acknowledge what someone is feeling, thinking, and carrying around.

You'll know someone needs you to put empathy before information when they're communicating a lot of emotion. Empathy works so well because it dampens the emotional charge someone is feeling, creates a space of safety, and opens the door for deeper, honest communication. In the end, that's all most of us want.

YOUR ROAD TO YES!

I've worked with some people who tend to lead, love, and communicate more from their head space. They want to have empathy, but it doesn't come naturally to them at this moment in their life. The formula I teach them for communicating with empathy is the following:

Of course you feel _____ [*name the emotion(s)*], because _____ [*describe the actions causing the emotion(s)*].

So if I'm talking to a mom who is venting about everything she's going through during the COVID pandemic, then I might say, "Of course, you're overwhelmed and exhausted because it doesn't feel like you ever get a break from the craziness going on. You're juggling your career, being a good mom, dealing with virtual school instruction, and COVID outbreaks at daycare that keep pulling staff and kids out. Every day feels like a new challenge, a new struggle, and it's just exhausting."

Watch someone nod their head and be overcome with relief when you respond this way. You've communicated in a way that made them say, "YES!" That is empathy.

Empathy can be hard because we live in a world where we rush around being busy. Empathy requires us to slow down, deeply listen to someone's experience, and not feel the need to solve anything for them immediately. It's easier and quicker to jump in with your perspective, tell others what they need to do based on your experience, and feel good about the value you just contributed to the conversation. The problem with that approach is that we often dismiss what they're feeling, believe our solution is the one right solution that will work for them, and don't empower them to develop their own choices on moving forward in their lives. Though we demonstrated this behavior with good intentions, it serves us more than it does the other person. People don't need fixing; they need to be heard. It's this level of intentionality that makes us team players.

Every day allows you to provide empathy to someone. Remember: empathy doesn't require you to have any answers. It simply invites you to show up and acknowledge someone's experience. That's how we build trust.

COMMIT TO AVAILABILITY

My pastor once shared that when someone is going through a hard time, many of us default to the response, "Call me if you need anything." He challenged us to stop saying that and explained that you're putting the responsibility for action back on the people who are already emotionally fatigued. As a result, they rarely call. Leadership is more than accessibility. It goes further than just having an "open-door policy." The goal is not to only be accessible when someone needs us. The goal is to be available even when they don't.

I coached an executive who wanted to figure out how to build better relationships with people at work. She talked about how empathetic and compassionate she was with people outside of work, but those same behaviors don't always translate back into the organization. She noted how she sometimes came across as aloof, disconnected, and straightforward in the workplace. I asked her what was causing her to show up as a different person. She reiterated how busy she was with the work. As a result of her busyness, she might not always come across as approachable or available. She made it clear to others that she was accessible when they needed her. She would remind them to just come to her office door. She said if it bothered them that she continued to work and multitask, they could tell her they needed her to focus on them and make her stop. We discussed that it's not other people's responsibility to manage our behavior. People who lack confidence or those in lower positions might not feel comfortable speaking up and telling you that they need you to be present for them. She noted she was always there for others when they were going through a challenging time. That's when her compassion was at its best. However, she realized that could come across as transactional. She highlighted she wanted people to know she was there for them even when they didn't need her. We brainstormed the difference between accessibility versus availability. Availability takes a few minutes each day to genuinely say hello to people. It resists the urge to rush and allows you to be part of the conversation. These small but meaningful micro-moments of trust-building are necessary. They slowly build comfort and confidence inside the relationship, which helps us when we engage in the more difficult moments.

Leaders make themselves available when they check in with their team for no reason other than to see how things are going, when they're "all in" while communicating, and when they provide positive and constructive feedback when appropriate.

Availability doesn't mean you have unfettered access to my immediate attention. It means I will always prioritize and be intentional about checking in with you, so you don't feel you put in most of the effort. Availability is my commitment to you that we will create a regular space to talk and learn from each other.

BE A TEAM PLAYER

One of the most important lessons I learned from marching in The Cavaliers Drum and Bugle Corps is that trust is a team sport. Part of being a great team player is encouraging those on the team because one day, you'll find yourself tired, frustrated, and in need of that support. Towards the end of our season in 2000, I specifically remember that my knee kept giving out at one of our practices. The guy next to me looks over and says, "Justin. You got this! You've done this so many times before. I know it's hard, but you can do it." This small but significant moment of encouragement is what I needed to hear. And he was right: I could do it. I did, and together we went on to win the gold medal at the world championships that year. Sometimes, being encouraged can give people the strength to keep pushing on. World-class teams show up and do that for each other.

TRUST IS A TEAM SPORT.

Shelly Behrens is the field hockey coach at Millersville University. She understands that trust is a team sport, so she helps cultivate trust by creating the space for relevant feedback and recognition. At the end of practice, all the players get together and quickly answer one question: "Who made you better today?" They respond by saying

something like, "Pillar, you made me better today because you
_____. Thank you." When their grades come out, Shelly
also sends text messages to her players to recognize their efforts and
remind them that she is there for them. Shelly's leadership teaches
her players that trusting relationships are built on constructive
feedback and recognition, which they will carry with them off the
field into every part of their lives.

Alison Beard recently interviewed actress and director Robin Wright.
One of the questions she asked was, "Hollywood's not an industry
known for patience and humility. How do you navigate that?"
Robin responded by saying, "The most important thing when you're
directing is to show kindness. It creates an energy on the set, where
anyone can say, 'I don't know the answer to that question. Let's have
a discussion. Let's collaborate. You bring your ideas to the table. I'll
bring mine. And let's decide what's best for the project.'" Robin's
collaborative nature makes people feel like they're part of a team.
They can surrender their egos, be vulnerable, and co-create a better
product because of everyone's contributions.

I once coached a manager who had some limiting behaviors she
needed to address if she wanted to move up in the organization.
The main issue was she never came across as a team player during
meetings and when addressing her concerns with people in higher
positions. During my first meeting with her, she acknowledged that
she often gets judgmental and jumps straight to her ego. She's not
one to be quiet, and her intensity gets the best of her. The framing
of her message turned people off and ultimately started limiting her
opportunities. I remember asking her, "What would it sound like to
still speak up and share your honest opinion and do it in a way that
made people believe you had the company's best interest in mind?"
She wasn't sure how. Her fear was becoming a "yes person" who
acquiesced to whatever leadership wanted. I reassured her that no
one wanted her to become a "yes person." They just wanted her to
become a team player. That required her to reframe her messages
differently.

Ways to communicate as a team player include framing your
message with something you know to be true, using inclusive

language like "we/our," and asking a question out of curiosity and interest versus judgment and condemnation. Check out the difference in the following messages and then decide which ones come across more as someone who is a team player.

Judgment and Condemnation	Curiosity and Interest
We do this every time. We make decisions that make it harder for our teams to be successful.	I know being a workplace where people feel like family is important to us…so I'm curious how this new policy will impact that. I'd love to hear what you all think.
We don't have the resources to do this successfully.	Technology innovation is one of our strategic priorities for the year…and it seems this is a step in the right direction. What additional resources will we need to launch this successfully?
You all never consider our perspectives when making these types of decisions, and then we have to communicate them to the team.	I know we didn't arrive at this decision lightly…Can you help us understand what went into making this decision, so we communicate appropriately?

Framing your message, as shown above, doesn't mean you can't be direct and share your honest feelings. However, it does challenge you to focus on how you say it and the timing in which you deliver it. That's part of being an emotionally intelligent leader.

Finally, being a great team player means you intentionally bring like-minded people together so that they can build emotional connections. Those emotional connections get people more engaged and invested in the brand. Peloton and Harley Davidson are masters at this. Both brands created the space for their existing customers to interact. Peloton riders can high-five each other during rides, get shout-outs from the instructors during live classes, and video-chat with a friend during a class. Harley Davidson has chapter meet-ups, communal bike rallies across the world, donation drives, and plenty of merchandise riders can wear to display their love for the brand. These interactions move people from customers to loyal superfans who do most of the marketing for the company.

All five examples highlight actions a team player would demonstrate if focused on building trust: encourage others, provide relevant feedback and recognition, genuinely collaborate, frame your message as a team player, and bring people together.

SPEND QUALITY TIME TOGETHER

We must spend quality time together if people in the workplace or any relationship are to feel like they're part of a team. You can't build trust with people you do not know. A common question on employee engagement surveys is, "Do I have a best friend at work?" Companies ask that question because they know that you're less likely to leave if you enjoy the people you work with. Leaders have a fundamental responsibility to help employees get to know each other through work and outside work.

Back when I worked for Yum! Brands, my boss told me they wanted me to go to Russia and teach a leadership workshop. I was like, "Thanks for the opportunity, but I'm going to have to pass." I had no interest in going to Russia by myself. After a lot of conversations about concerns and what this opportunity would look like, they finally agreed to send someone else on the team with me. Let me tell you; you really get to know someone when you're planning a trip to Russia with them! I learned about my team member's family. I witnessed her expertise and insights as we planned the training material. And I got to experience how comfortable her presence made others feel. On another note, I also witnessed her spend all of our money at an underground club in Moscow, leading us to walk an hour back to the hotel in the snow. We earned a deeper level of respect and personal connection because of the work we were able to do together.

YOUR ROAD TO YES!

It doesn't take a trip to Russia to implement this idea of taking people with you, but it does take effort. Regardless of their titles and positions in companies, the best leaders use their presence to create an inclusive environment. They invite people to participate in activities, whether lunch, a gathering outside of work, or a meeting. They ask people for their ideas and feedback. They check in and genuinely learn about others.

CREATE PERSONALIZED TOUCHPOINTS

When I joined Yum! Brands in 2012, I quickly received a bouquet of cookies at my house with a handwritten note from my manager welcoming me to the team. I felt valued! At every team meeting, recognition was given to individuals for their efforts and then displayed for everyone in the building to see. People felt seen! A few months later, the makeshift "marching band" circled my cubical while shaking tambourines and cheering. I was designated a "culture hero" and received a tricycle I could ride around the office for a month. The workplace was fun!

Former PepsiCo CEO Indra Nooyi wrote personal letters to the parents of her senior executives. She acknowledged that parents have a lot to do with their children's success, so she wanted them to know how much she appreciated their contributions. She thanked them for the gift of their child at PepsiCo. Those personal letters made her staff feel appreciated, and it made the parents proud.

In one of his viral videos, Kid President said we should treat everyone like it's their birthday. What an awesome idea! If we did that, we would let people know how much they mean to us, get them a meaningful gift, and be present. My sister is awesome at creating little birthday gift bags for people. I didn't inherit that talent, and it gives me anxiety thinking about what to get my staff and clients. I needed something that would help take away the anxiety and help me personalize the gifts when I decided to give them. In my organization, staff and clients fill out a personalized recognition form that tells us their birthday, family makeup, favorite things like snacks, charities, places to shop, and things they can't get enough of. We send the clients that have completed the form an email on their birthday reminding them how the world changed the day they were born. I also mail them a handwritten card. The gifts we send throughout the year are tailored to the items they like.

TRUST IS PERSONAL.

All these examples highlight that trust is personal. When we take the time to personalize our efforts, we meet people where they are. When we meet people where they are, we make them feel less alone in the world. It's there, in that space of togetherness, that we build trust.

YES! TO TOGETHERNESS

The best leaders show up every day at both work and home and use their presence to make others feel less alone in the world. I don't know if every person in your life will be in a place to receive that love and kindness, but I know it's worth the effort. This level of intentionality allows you to form meaningful, long-lasting relationships.

- What relationship(s) in your life would benefit from a stronger sense of togetherness?
- What can you do this week to make those individuals feel less alone?
- If a high-performer replaced you for a day and made others feel valued, what would that high-performer be doing differently than you are now?

People can occasionally see past our inability to be transparent and tactful in communicating, but they will always expect us to be team players. The road traveled should never be a lonely one. Your presence makes all the difference.

SUMMARY

- Togetherness is your ability to make people feel like they're part of a team.
- Teamwork is really a form of trust.
- Trust is built when everyone is focused on each other's survival and success.
- Six Ways Leaders Create a Sense of Togetherness
  1. Demonstrate Consistency
  2. Put Empathy Before Information
  3. Commit to Availability
  4. Be a Team Player
  5. Spend Quality Time Together
  6. Create Personalized Touchpoints
- Empathy is the willingness to see beyond yourself and acknowledge what someone is feeling, thinking, and carrying around.
- Empathy formula:
  - Of course you feel _____ [name the emotion(s)],
  - Because _____ [describe the actions causing the emotion(s)].
- Trust is personal.
- Togetherness requires you to be able to answer "YES!" to the following question:
  Do I make people feel less alone in the world?

CHAPTER SIX

FACTORS THAT ERODE TRUST

The more we build trust,
The more we build resilience
For what can be healed.

YOUR ROAD TO YES!

Your presence is your greatest gift, and how you show up will determine whether people trust you or not. Every action you take represents your awareness at the moment, not necessarily your highest self. When you're tired, stressed, and emotionally depleted, your bullshit meter will be a lot lower than when you're feeling rested and refreshed. As a result, you might respond in ways that aren't consistent with how you normally show up.

YOUR
PRESENCE
IS YOUR
GREATEST GIFT.

I remember being in the Atlanta airport security line. TSA's new system required customers to grab a bin, place only one bag inside it, and wait for the automatic belt to push their belongings through before walking to the X-ray machine. There were no signs on this system, so if you'd never seen this system in use before, you wouldn't know what to do. This woman beside me placed her belongings on the belt and walked away. The TSA agent warned, "Stop! Wait until you push your bags forward!" and then rolled her eyes.

I had just flown nine hours from Hawaii to Atlanta, and I was sleep-deprived. No one deserved to be talked to this way. So I said, "Ma'am...she just doesn't understand that."

The TSA agent snapped back, "Well, I wasn't talking to you! You want to start with me today too?"

You know that went over well. I know bullying is one of my triggers, and I have no tolerance for it. I knew my response might land me in a back room somewhere, but I had three hours before my next flight, so I figured I'd still make it on time. I stayed calm and said, "Not particularly. But you could just be kind and live the values of what you all stand for."

She said, "I better just walk away..." and she did.

We both walked away from that situation with a negative view of each other. I'm sure she thought I was a jerk, and I thought she should find another job. We didn't have any prior positive experiences to balance this one moment; therefore, this moment is how we would define each other. Trust never had a chance.

TRUST IS ERODED WHEN THE IMPACT OF SOMEONE'S ACTIONS OUTWEIGHS THE AMOUNT OF EMOTIONAL CONNECTION PREVIOUSLY BUILT IN THE RELATIONSHIP.

Examples like this happen every day. Some of our relationships have a lot of history and can survive an isolated moment where we don't show up our best. Other relationships have no prior history, and—*right or wrong*—people write you off from the start. Trust is eroded when the impact of someone's actions outweighs the amount of emotional connection previously built in the relationship. If you work for a boss you appreciate and admire, but then at one point she doesn't follow through on a commitment she made to you, you're likely to show some grace and understand she made a mistake. However, you might question her intentions and lose trust if you think she passed you over for a job you deserved and made you believe you would be a good fit.

Each relationship has a different level of trust tolerance based on its history. Trust tolerance is what you're willing to endure and let go of before you lose trust in someone. Your best friend might demonstrate the same behavior as your boss, but because you have a more emotional history with your best friend, you might not detach from that relationship as quickly as you would your boss. The more we build trust in our relationships, the more we build the trust tolerance for what the relationship can survive in the future.

And here's the honest reality: *time breaks everything!* You're human. You're going to have a bad day. You're going to say something you don't mean at some point. You're going to unintentionally trigger someone. Your actions aren't going to live up to your or someone else's expectations. You're going to disappoint people in relationships at some point. It's the cost of being in long-term relationships where we stop trying to play a part, let our guard down, and allow someone else to see us trying just to figure life out.

YOUR ROAD TO YES!

It's often because we care so much about the relationship that it hurts so deeply when the trust is broken. But broken doesn't mean over. Instead, broken challenges us to see things differently, engage in some meaningful conversations, and decide how we put things back together.

All relationship troubles result from a trust breakdown. Those breakdowns can usually be traced back to an issue in one or more of the three trust factors: transparency, tact, or togetherness. Sometimes it can be one big action that erodes the foundation of a relationship, like a manager putting an employee on a performance improvement plan without any prior communication (transparency issue), a friend blowing up in the middle of a difficult conversation (tact issue), or a partner cheating

ALL RELATIONSHIP TROUBLES RESULT FROM A TRUST BREAKDOWN.

(togetherness issue). Other times, it's a series of actions, like not communicating in your relationship, always dismissing or shaming someone when they try to communicate with you, and not making the other person in the relationship feel special and valued, that ultimately leads to the lack of trust in a relationship.

A friend once reminded me of a powerful quote from Robin Sharma: "The way we do small things determines the way we do everything." So if someone is at a point in their life where they feel they need to hide their pictures, phone, where they've been, or why they didn't call, they will also hide the big things from you and the relationship. That behavior has nothing to do with you. You just need to be with someone ready to be transparent in their journey.

One of the biggest mistakes we make when trust is eroded is that we don't talk about the issue(s) soon enough. This is just another reason I say that silence is the biggest threat to trust. Organizational psychologist Adam Grant said, "It's uncomfortable to end a friendship or pause a partnership. It's unkind to stop responding… Silence doesn't avoid conflict. It offloads it onto the person who's ghosted." If you value trust and believe in its merits, you must value closure over comfort. Trust challenges us to engage in conversations that aren't easy but necessary.

I once had an assistant who I respected and whose work I appreciated. Over time, I noticed that the level of detail that made her so successful in her role was no longer present. It was taking longer for the work to get done, and she wasn't as personal in her responses to others. I initiated a couple of coaching conversations to address what I noticed, but nothing changed over the next few weeks. I found myself getting frustrated. I felt that she didn't have my back as she did before. Her work product was no longer consistent, and I had to check up on things. I don't want to be the silently bitter person, so I brought the topic back up. I trusted the relationship could handle the difficult conversation. I told her that I valued everything she had done for the business. We were better because of her, but I'd noticed that she wasn't performing with the same consistency, and we needed to figure this out together. She explained how her other full-time job that she had just started required way more energy than she thought it would. I appreciated the honesty.

We both decided it would be best for her to transition out of the role. Here's where trust matters! She became part of the transition process. She helped me hire her replacement. She stayed on an extra month and made sure to train that person. We were a team throughout the whole process. I think that is a testament to our trust in each other. Had there been a lack of trust in our relationship, I think she would have only given me short notice. I would have felt blindsided, and the business would have suffered. Trust allowed us to create closure in her role but maintain a relationship moving forward. That's a win-win for everyone.

TRUST IS EVERYONE'S RESPONSIBILITY IN A RELATIONSHIP AND ORGANIZATION.

Trust is everyone's responsibility in a relationship and organization. Managers are responsible for building trust in themselves and with each person on their team and then for helping foster the space for trust to grow.

Some of the most common mistakes managers make that erode trust include:

1. Lack of follow-through
2. Blindsides team members
3. Shares confidential information
4. Micromanages
5. Undermanages
6. Rewards bad behavior
7. Doesn't take genuine interest in others
8. Inconsistent
9. Doesn't recognize others
10. Doesn't manage intensity

SIX RED FLAGS ON TRUST

We build high levels of trust when a relationship feels like a partnership. We are both passengers on the journey. We enjoy and seek out each other's company. We value the strengths and differences each other brings, and we have fun together.

No one likes a back-seat driver. These people often feel like they need to be in control. When they're not, they criticize the other person's choices, make audible sounds of disproval, stomp the imaginary brake pedal, and explain where to go when the other person already knows the directions. These actions don't feel helpful. They feel judgmental, and it's exhausting for both people. This is not how we develop trust in our relationships. I believe we all have the potential to be back-seat drivers. This behavior is always rooted in our ego and the need to be right, heard, and in control. Our ego often prevents us from connecting with ourselves and each other. With this awareness, we can let go of being the only driver in a relationship and make choices that allow us to both be passengers and build trust.

Below are six red flags that indicate trust might be an ongoing issue when someone consistently demonstrates them. These behaviors are driven by ego. We cannot be team players or build trust when we're focused only on ourselves.

Red Flag #1:
Thinks Everyone Else is the Problem

A company where I delivered some leadership workshops once called me up and asked if I could coach a woman leader who they believed in but was demonstrating some self-defeating behaviors. Of course, I was up for it, but I told them that she had to be included in the process. The woman was reluctant, but she decided to give it a try. In our first session, I asked her why she was here and what she wanted to get out of this process. She spent a good amount of time blaming everyone in her life for everything else that was going wrong. Her boss wasn't a great leader. The organization's president was the wrong fit for the company. The people under her didn't seem to care anymore, and she wanted to work with people who had passion. She didn't have a great relationship with her family, and she wasn't sure if the town she was in was the right fit any longer.

I paused. "Wow!" I said. "That must feel overwhelming and emotionally exhausting." She laughed and agreed. I asked if I could share an observation with her based on years of coaching experience. I said, "I've found that when everyone else is the problem, we're often the problem."

It is so much easier to blame everyone else in life for what they're doing wrong, for how they're showing up, and how they're "contributing" to our disappointment. This behavior is safe because it prevents us from owning our part in the dysfunction of any relationship.

I remember walking into therapy in my twenties, blaming my emotional turmoil on my family and ex. Sitting on the sofa across from the therapist, I vented, cried, and listed my lifetime of grievances. I then walked out of that session thinking, "Oh shit, maybe I'm part of the problem." And that awareness was some of the most rewarding mental clarity I've had in my life.

Someone who blames everyone else in life is often unable at that moment to see how they've demonstrated the same behaviors as others. They lack empathy, see life and people through a pessimistic lens, and avoid taking any accountability for how their presence has contributed to the current situation. It's hard, if not impossible, to build trust with someone unable to take an honest, vulnerable look at themselves from time to time.

> Guiding Question:
> *What if I'm the problem?*

Red Flag #2:
Believes Their Truth is the Only Truth

I had a mentor who once told me, "Own your truth, but know that your truth is not the only truth." As someone who teaches leadership presence, I believe confidence is important. I also know owning your voice is foundational to growing your self-confidence. But we don't have to sacrifice and minimize others' voices in owning ours.

How many of you remember the infamous moment that Taylor Swift won her 2009 Video Music Award for Best Video by a Female Artist? As she starts to accept the award, Kanye West gets on stage and shares why Beyonce deserved the award over Taylor. He states, "I'mma let you finish, but Beyonce had one of the best videos of all time! One of the best videos of all time!" Taylor stands there stunned, feeling dismissed, the moment ruined.

Kanye West—or Ye as he is now known—was wrong for many reasons. He took the spotlight away from Taylor and made it all about himself. He had no regard for the impact his presence had on Taylor, the VMAs, his brand, or the audience. He believed his truth was the only truth, and he would do whatever it took at that moment to be heard.

And here's the ugly reality: we've all been Kanye before. I know it's hard to accept. I cringed a little when I wrote it as well. We've all had that moment in a conversation where we were focused more on being right than listening and trying to understand. In our desire to be right, we miss the chance to collaborate and understand things from a different perspective. We've all interjected something at a time that wasn't appropriate. Our ego makes us want to stand up at that exact moment and prove to others why they're wrong. Your ego will fool you into believing this is the only choice. You might win the conversation and the moment, but you will sacrifice trust in the process. It's never worth it.

> Guiding Question:
> *What are they trying to tell me that maybe I'm not hearing?*

Red Flag #3:
Expects You to Earn Their Trust But Doesn't Reciprocate

Somewhere along the way, I heard a famous speaker ask, "What is the number one action that keeps couples together and happy for long periods?" I love the wording of that question because the speaker acknowledged how you could be married and alone. You could be married and miserable. So what keeps couples together and happy? The answer came out to be "giving." Couples that were happy and stayed together kept giving to each other where other couples had stopped. They were raising kids, focused on their careers, and had often unconsciously reprioritized each other out of importance. They were so busy being busy that they stopped demonstrating the very action that allowed them to develop trust and love from the beginning.

You might find yourself in a relationship in the future where the person expects you to earn their trust and make them feel special and valued, but then you're left thinking, "What about me?" Healthy relationships built on trust are never one-sided. Both people give. And when someone is going through something and maybe can't provide as much as they did before, the other person keeps giving anyway. If it gets to the point where you feel you're being taken advantage of, then love the relationship enough to have a conversation about what is happening and what you both need moving forward.

In leadership, we know one of the top drivers of employee engagement is recognition. It's one of the easiest and simplest ways to make employees feel valued, but it doesn't happen consistently in many organizations. It's no longer enough to give a paycheck and think that's how you're adding value to the relationship. That would be like going home and saying, "Well, I paid the mortgage payment, so my wife and kids know I love them." Creating safety and security in any relationship is the bare minimum for creating trust. Making people feel seen and valued takes trust to a much deeper level. Executive leaders and managers who want to build a culture of trust and belonging must find ways to constantly give to their team members and make them feel like they're not alone and that their work is appreciated.

It's hard to be in a relationship with someone who consistently expects you to earn and prove your trustworthiness. Everything you do is scored against their insecurities and expectations, and you will have a hard time living up to it. However, if both people focus on giving trust, the earning will automatically happen.

> Guiding Question:
> *What can I do right now to build trust in this relationship?*

Red Flag #4:
Uses Intensity to Shut Down Effective Communication

In my certification on difficult conversations, I learned that many of us have a default we go to in challenging situations. We use this behavior as our coping mechanism because we've learned that it serves us. I'm a recovering yeller. Someone could walk away, and I would follow them, saying, "Oh, we're not done talking about this!" My intensity would often intimidate and exhaust other people, so they'd end the conversation quickly. I left feeling I'd won, but I had actually lost their trust in the relationship. My sister's intensity comes out in the complete opposite way. She bails out of conversations and will often cry. When she cries, others usually try to console her or feel bad and wrap up the conversation quicker. My partner gets quiet during the uncomfortable conversations. That's the most brutal reaction for me to deal with. I'll say, "So it looks like you don't want to talk about this right now?" And he'll stare.

We will all have moments where we get emotionally hijacked, and our intensity gets the best of us. However, this should not be in every difficult conversation. If someone has a pattern of using intensity to shut down effective communication, this needs to be addressed. There is a space for anger, crying, and silence. But none of those emotions should be used to discipline and reprimand someone.

Intensity is the antithesis of transparency. If you know the other person has a pattern of responding with hostility, you're likely to withhold information, sugarcoat what needs to be said, or wait too long to bring up a conversation. You do a disservice to the trust in a relationship when you prioritize comfort over a necessary conversation.

> ### Guiding Question:
> *What would it sound like to communicate my perspective with tact?*

Red Flag #5:
Lacks Empathy

I believe empathy is one of the most essential skills for a healthy relationship. And I'm telling you that as someone who lacked empathy for most of my twenties and early thirties.

Years ago, I had an argument with my friend. He was a lawyer and routinely stoic. As the conversation went on, things just got more heated. As the intensity increased, I dug in. At some point, I looked over, and he started to cry. I stopped. I hugged him and apologized, but the damage was done. My desire to be right caused me to put on emotional blinders and prevented me from hearing what he was trying to tell me. He didn't need me to agree with him. He needed me to say, "Thank you for sharing that with me. I don't think I realized it came across that way, and I could have handled that differently." Or "I can see how my response would be overwhelming and make you feel dismissed."

Empathy is the ability to see beyond yourself, so you can understand and acknowledge someone else's perspective. Empathy demonstrates that we're genuinely people-focused and can work well with others. It is a driving factor that allows us to make a space feel safe and have more meaningful conversations with each other.

I don't believe there is a one-size-fits-all leadership approach, but empathy is an important skill for any leader's effectiveness. The more people feel heard and acknowledged, the more trust they feel towards you. When there's more trust, people are more likely to be candid, engaged, and team players. Having empathy doesn't mean we don't hold people accountable. There is a space for both, and the best leaders demonstrate empathy while also addressing who did what.

EMPATHY IS THE ABILITY TO SEE BEYOND YOURSELF, SO YOU CAN UNDERSTAND AND ACKNOWLEDGE SOMEONE ELSE'S PERSPECTIVE.

Being in any relationship with someone unable or unwilling to show empathy will feel transactional and lonely. You'll desperately want to feel seen, but they will often resort to "fixing" you or the situation. They will tell you what to do based on their prior experiences and insights. Instead of feeling heard and empowered, you leave feeling unheard and sometimes even more confused. I often remind myself that "people don't need to be fixed; they need to be heard." Empathy is always the starting place for effective communication.

Guiding Question:
What can I acknowledge about this person's feelings or perspective?

Red Flag #6:
Lacks Self Confidence

Confidence is our ability to respect and believe in ourselves while accepting both our strengths and weaknesses, and it's so important in relationships because what you believe about yourself will come out in your actions.

When someone lacks self-confidence, they often hustle for other people's permission, approval, and validation. Someone with low self-confidence might lack assertiveness, hesitate to say what they think and feel, hesitate to set boundaries, or silence themselves on the things that matter. Other times, someone with a lack of self-confidence will outsource their decision-making. They're slow to go after the things they want. Low confidence can also cause an individual to foster feelings of resentment and jealousy as they become consumed with others' success.

I once coached an executive who struggled with her self-confidence. She told me during our initial meeting, "I'm really good at relationships and making people think I'm good at my job, but am I?" For those surprised by that comment, it's a common occurrence for both men and women. The core of almost every issue I've ever coached executives on typically comes back to a lack of confidence. This high-performing client was a self-proclaimed "people-pleaser." Unfortunately, she was trying to please everyone else in life, and it cost a little bit of herself every time. She was vulnerable and authentic during our conversations. She acknowledged that she placed her confidence in her looks when she was younger. Then she got pregnant, gained weight, and things changed. She didn't feel confident anymore. We discussed that this was because she tried tying her confidence to external factors, which never works. We spent three months exploring who she was at her best, what made her a badass, and what value she brought to her organization and home. Over time, she started investing in herself more. She spoke up more at work with her ideas. She communicated more clearly and openly with her husband. She came to terms with her weaknesses and permitted herself to be okay with them as long as they did not derail her relationships and career. And she stopped trying to own how people felt when she spoke up. Instead, she allowed them to take responsibility for their feelings. Towards the end of our coaching relationship, she told me, "I learned that the world wouldn't end if I stood up for myself." She learned to create more room in her life for herself, and everyone else benefited. That is the power of confidence in a relationship. Confidence is not hustling for the world to like you. Confidence is liking yourself regardless of whether others do or not.

Guiding Question:
What action would I take if I owned my confidence?

THE WEAPONIZATION OF TRUST

There are few greater grievances than the mishandling of trust. Each day, you have the chance to pay attention to the small but meaningful moments, to assess those you feel safe with and those who might be weaponizing your trust.

If others' actions make you believe they have your back, you likely feel confident investing in the relationship. On the other hand, if their actions cause you to raise an eyebrow, you should ask yourself if they're mishandling your trust.

The weaponization of trust happens when people consciously or unconsciously take the information you've shared with them and use it for their personal gain—whether to get a laugh, hold you hostage to your past, control you, force you in or out of a relationship, get ahead of you, or prevent you from getting ahead.

Perhaps we've even weaponized someone else's trust. I remember being at dinner with friends in my early twenties. We were all joking, and at some point, I brought up something about my best friend in the room that he had shared only with me. It got a laugh, but that action sent a warning shot to my friend. We had a big talk about what I'd done, and I had to own up that I had acted wrongly. I mishandled his trust, and he deserved better from me.

THE WEAPONIZATION OF TRUST HAPPENS WHEN PEOPLE CONSCIOUSLY OR UNCONSCIOUSLY TAKE THE INFORMATION YOU'VE SHARED WITH THEM AND USE IT FOR THEIR PERSONAL GAIN

This mishandling of trust also happens professionally. I've experienced a manager tell me something confidential that their employee told them. The employee trusted their manager not to share that information.

Only you will know if one's actions are the product of an isolated incident or a reoccurring pattern of behavior. In my leadership book, *Bold New You*, I refer to individuals who continuously weaponize other people's trust as "emotional terrorists":

"Emotional terrorists are dangerous and destructive to relationships because their righteous indignation becomes an ideology that allows them to justify their bad behavior. Instead of co-creating a relationship that works for both people, they abuse others to create a relationship that works solely for themselves. They use the most sensitive and vulnerable things they have learned about you against you. They take the trust you put in them, and they turn around and use it as a psychological weapon to whittle you into submission and out of your own self-worth."

The weaponization of trust happens in workplaces every day. If you regularly experience any of the following situations, it might be happening in your organization right now.:

1. You feel you can't show up as your authentic self.
2. Your manager only engages with you when they need something.
3. Someone uses sarcasm or humor at your expense.
4. You're not receiving the feedback and coaching you need to succeed.
5. You've been written off for any type of future advancement.
6. People at work gossip about each other.
7. Someone continuously apologizes but keeps demonstrating the same behavior.

If you feel someone is weaponizing your trust, it's imperative that you have a conversation, express your feelings, and set a clear boundary about what you need moving forward. If the person is interested in building a mutually satisfying relationship, they will respond accordingly. However, if they show no effort in earning your trust, get out with your self-worth and confidence intact. You cannot and should not negotiate with an emotional terrorist.

FINAL THOUGHT:

We are all going to make mistakes in relationships from time to time. We are all going to erode someone's trust or be in a relationship where we feel like trust is slipping away. But when we're aware of the factors that erode trust, we can recognize them more quickly and respond in a healthier way.

We all have reasons not to trust others, but we must hang on to all the reasons we should. I would rather spend my life believing in the goodness of people and being occasionally proved wrong than walking around numb to the pleasures, pitfalls, and rewards that come with trusting.

CHAPTER SIX
SUMMARY

- Your presence is your greatest gift.
- Trust is eroded when the impact of someone's actions outweighs the amount of emotional connection previously built in the relationship.
- Trust tolerance is what you're willing to endure and let go of before you lose trust in someone.
- The more we build trust in our relationships, the more we build the trust tolerance for what the relationship can survive in the future.
- All relationship troubles are a result of a trust breakdown.
- Six Red Flags on Trust:
  1. Thinks everyone else in the problem
  2. Believes their truth is the only truth
  3. Expects you to earn their trust but doesn't reciprocate
  4. Uses intensity to shut down effective communication
  5. Lacks empathy
  6. Lacks self-confidence
- The weaponization of trust happens when people consciously or unconsciously take the information you've shared with them and use it for their personal gain.

YOUR ROAD TO YES!

HOW TO REPAIR TRUST ONCE IT'S BROKEN

The bridge between your
Suffering and your healing
Is through forgiveness.

Trust is the unwavering belief that you have my back. When we break one another's trust, we break an agreement. It is a gut punch that leaves us feeling alone and afraid. It is an employee being let down by their manager and unsure what this means for her future and how she will pay her bills. It's a boss feeling like they can't depend on their employee anymore. It's a kid feeling like he can't talk to his parents about what he's going through. It's a couple not living up to each other's expectations and wondering if being alone is the same as the loneliness they're currently experiencing. Broken trust makes us feel vulnerable. That's why it's easier for some to just bail on the relationship when it gets difficult. Our willingness to talk through things creates intimacy, honesty, and transparency in our relationships.

Beginnings are easy. Staying together is the difficult part. National studies have consistently shown that 50 percent of first-time marriages will end in divorce. The percentages are even higher for second and third-time marriages. I would like to think we're all engaged when we first enter a relationship or a new organization. You remember how that "newness" feels. You're excited. You're open to learning and trying new things. You talk about the experience with your friends. You have a newfound sense of hope for what the future could bring. Perhaps, in the beginning, we have a little bit stronger faith in each other. But then there comes the point when the newness wears off, and the relationship doesn't feel as fun or spontaneous as it once did. That's when the real work begins.

> BEGINNINGS ARE EASY. STAYING TOGETHER IS THE DIFFICULT PART.

I think that's why people say, "Love isn't a feeling; it's a commitment." Are we willing to stay committed to the relationship even when we might not feel as seen, valued, special, or supported?

Commitment doesn't mean we have to put up with bad behavior. It means we're committed to discussing what's happening in the relationship and figuring out the next steps together.

I recently worked out with a friend who said the moment someone betrays his trust, he's out. He even quoted my favorite poet, Maya Angelou: "When someone shows you who they are, believe them the first time." I struggle with this advice and how to interpret it. Part of me wants to be like, "Hell yes! Don't put up with anything and walk out the moment they show you who they *really* are." The other part of me hopes that someone will show me a little grace and compassion when I mess up. If you watch the video clip where Maya Angelou and Oprah Winfrey discuss this life lesson, Maya talks about not taking twenty-nine times to learn a lesson.

We need to believe that's who that person is earlier on in the relationship. However, I don't think you ever know who someone is by the "first time." One moment does not define our pattern of behavior. We've all had moments where we did not show up as our best. We've all lied, but that doesn't make you a chronic liar. We've all dropped the ball on something at work, but that doesn't make you unreliable. We've all said something the wrong way, but that doesn't make you someone who always lacks tact and bullies people to get what you want. Those incidents are isolated moments, and we can use them to inform us, express our feelings, clarify boundaries, or do nothing and see if it becomes a pattern for how we, or someone else, show up consistently. Maya Angelou never said, "When someone shows you who they are, pack your stuff and walk out the first time." If we bail out whenever someone shows us who they are, we will struggle with any long-term relationship. When you constantly look for a reason not to trust someone, you'll find it.

IS THIS A PATTERN, OR IS THIS JUST A MOMENT?

A great question to ask ourselves when someone does something that impacts our trust in them is, "Is this a pattern, or is this just a moment?" If it's just an isolated moment where someone didn't show up as their best, maybe we can give the person some grace, be willing to let stuff go, and check in and re-establish boundaries if needed. I recently watched the television series *Manifest* when one of the characters said, "Everyone deserves one free pass." Maybe this resonated differently because of where I am in my life right now, but all I could think about was, "How true!" If the incident is isolated, I'm more concerned with why you did it, what you need to acknowledge and learn, and what you'll commit to doing differently. Giving someone a free pass doesn't mean we absolve them of responsibility. It means we recognize their humanness and don't bail at the first sign of trouble.

However, I understand that nothing in life is that black and white. There are always situations and circumstances where providing a free pass is unhealthy. There are times when someone's actions are deal-breakers, and you must walk away immediately. You cannot stay with someone who violates your safety and security. When you do, you amputate your self-worth and sanity for another person. You'll always be the one left in pieces. No one is worth that choice, and any relationship worth having wouldn't want that from you.

When these isolated moments happen, we must be careful that we don't subconsciously turn them into someone's pattern and then see everything they do through that lens. When that happens, every action reinforces the story we have already told ourselves. No relationship can survive this type of fear story.

Humans are fallible. We're going to mess up. We're going to have moments where we disappoint others. You will do something, at some point, that erodes trust with someone else. It's then that you will need to rebuild trust. Let your motto be: We find a way through, or we find a way out, but we're not remaining stuck! Finding a way through won't always be easy, but it is possible. You must be willing to fight for the relationship with the same ferocity with which you're willing to walk away.

WE FIND A WAY THROUGH, OR WE FIND A WAY OUT, BUT WE'RE NOT REMAINING STUCK!

No one "right" process for repairing trust will work for every relationship. However, there are best practices that will better prepare and equip you if repairing trust is what both people in the relationship want to do. Below are the four steps to repairing broken trust.

FOUR STEPS TO REPAIRING TRUST:

1. Take ownership.
2. Renegotiate the relationship.
3. Ask for or extend forgiveness.
4. Demonstrate a change in behavior.

The four steps to repairing trust are *NOT* a linear process. They are all necessary, but the steps happen in different orders based on the relationship and situation. For example, sometimes, you'll need to forgive yourself before you're willing to take ownership. Sometimes you'll extend forgiveness to someone and then realize you'll need to go back and renegotiate the relationship again because you have more clarity about what you need and want to move forward. Other times, you'll want to take ownership and demonstrate a change in behavior before renegotiating what you both need from each other. The point is all four steps play a pivotal role in repairing trust, and how they play out in your relationship might be different than someone else's.

Let's explore these four steps to repairing trust in depth.

TAKE OWNERSHIP

Do you want to know someone's actual level of self-confidence and integrity? Don't worry about who they are when things are easy and going well. Instead, watch how they respond when they've hit bottom, when they've violated the beliefs of who they thought they were, and when their sense of security feels like it's crumbling away. I want to see that person. I want to witness if they retreat from vulnerability or use it as their mirror. I want to hear if they blame everyone else in the world for what's wrong or fall on the ground and take ownership of everything that led them to that singular moment. I want them to own their shit and then get up and realize they're still worthy of everything good in life. I want to be that person.

YOUR ROAD TO YES!

Ownership is not easy. It's risky and uncomfortable. That's why it's only reserved for the brave. When you take full ownership of your thoughts, feelings, and actions in each relationship, you choose to stop lying to yourself and express what is coming up for you to move forward in a healthy way. Ownership is about accepting full responsibility for your experience in the relationship.

OWNERSHIP IS ABOUT ACCEPTING FULL RESPONSIBILITY FOR YOUR EXPERIENCE IN THE RELATIONSHIP.

We all mess up sometimes in relationships. As Kid President once said, "The biggest mess up is not forgiving each other's mess-ups." You're not expected to be perfect. You're expected to be honest. You might not always get it right, but you can always commit to loving people enough to tell them the truth. Your ability to recover and build stronger levels of trust has a lot to do with your actions and how you handle the situation. You must take ownership of your experience in the relationship and how you contributed to the broken trust.

Taking ownership starts with yourself. You should spend quality time processing and working through your thoughts and feelings before placing them on someone else's shoulders. The more aware we are of our experience in the relationship, the better we communicate. The better we communicate, the greater our chance that we can work through any situation together. Ownership requires a high degree of emotional self-awareness and expression. You will be forced to step away from the busyness you've used as a coping mechanism to avoid dealing with what you need to deal with. You'll need time to slow down and answer some of the following questions:

- How am I contributing to the experience of trust or distrust in the relationship?
- How am I currently feeling in the relationship?
- How have I contributed to that feeling?
- What feelings and actions do I need to admit to myself?
- What is driving my choices in the relationship?

- What past patterns, if any, am I repeating?
- Who has been directly impacted by my actions?
- What feelings and actions do I need to acknowledge to the other person?

I met a woman at one of my speaking events who told me about a conversation she had with her therapist. Right before leaving one of her sessions, the therapist said, "What would happen if you chose just to love your dad?" For her to love the way she wanted and in a way that would honor the relationship, she would have to take ownership of everything she felt and lay all the broken pieces of her heart out for her father to see. She got home and dialed his number. As the phone rang, she anxiously hoped he would not pick up on the other end. He did. She immediately started to cry. Her dad stopped what he was doing and just listened for the first time in a long time. She explained how upset she was that he didn't make it to her son's graduation. She was angry that he had cancer. She laid it all the line and told him there were times she hated and resented him for what had happened in the past. She had stopped loving him for far too long, and she didn't want that to be their relationship. They both cried, and then through the tears came laughter and a bridge toward future conversations.

Let me demonstrate how this plays out in a professional setting as well. I had a friend who felt his manager acted differently toward him and made snide remarks on calls in front of other team members. The behavior started to worry my friend and sent him on an emotional rollercoaster about whether his job was on the line. Instead of stewing in it and making assumptions based on no facts, he sent his manager a text message asking if they could talk. They jumped on a call, and he immediately took ownership of his part in the relationship. He expressed how he felt like their relationship had recently changed, and he wanted to understand things from her perspective. She immediately apologized and reassured him his job was not on the line. She explained that she was getting a lot of heat from people above her on deadlines. She knew the team was already at capacity, and she wasn't sure how they would meet the company's goals. They both got off the phone with stronger awareness about what was going on, why each other was showing up in the relationship the way they were, and what they could do differently moving forward. He admitted that he probably would have gotten more defensive and just started detaching from the relationship had the conversation not happened. That would have been a lose-lose for everyone involved. By leaning into his fear and owning his emotions, he could create a more positive outcome and move forward differently.

Both stories illustrate that broken trust happens from a steady ripple of not showing up for each other. However, sometimes trust is broken because of one big action. Perhaps that one action was such a violation of trust that it caused a landslide where everything came crashing down. In a personal relationship, this could be infidelity, engaging inappropriately with people online, or lying. Professionally, this could look like going behind someone's back, taking credit for someone's work, sabotaging someone's career, or stealing. When this happens, the person who caused the act of betrayal must take ownership of what they did before the other person finds out on their own. The lies and denial of what happened often hurt people just as much as the actual betrayal of trust.

My dad is a very special person in my life. I admire the person he was and how he showed up for his friends and family. However, that doesn't mean he always got it right. He was human with his own baggage, insecurities, and traumatic upbringing he never fully worked through. When I was eighteen years old, my parents found out I was going to LGBTQ+ bars. My dad was getting ready for work one night, and we got into a huge fight. He didn't want me going to the bar, and in my stubborn way, I told him that wasn't his choice. Our voices kept getting louder. The tension in the room was palpable, and he cut through it when he yelled, "I fought in Vietnam for what I believe in, and I'll fight you over this—EVEN IF IT MEANS LOSING YOU."

There it was—the landslide. In just twenty-one words, a lifetime of trust started crumbling. How could one of the people who was supposed to love me the most, who talked a good game about unconditional love, just lay down a condition on what makes me worthy of belonging? Every ounce of security I had in my relationship with my father was shattered, and I was left alone to figure out what I was going to do. A few months later, he unexpectedly passed away.

I've never written about this story or shared it with many people. I don't want my dad remembered for just that one line. He was so much more than that. But he was also human and wrestling with his own prejudices and fears. And maybe part of our problem is that we don't share stories this real, this raw enough. My relationship with my dad wasn't all sprinkles on the cake. I use that analogy purposefully, and I hope he would laugh at it now. Our relationship was love tossed into a box of insecurities and two people just trying to figure a way to sort it all out.

After his death, I had to take ownership of everything I felt. I had to give myself permission to be hurt and find what he said as unacceptable. In time, I wrote him a letter, and there in that ink, I decided to leave my pain behind, grant him forgiveness, and use my voice to help people show up differently. It was then that I started to rebuild the trust with my father.

> WE HAVE CREATED A LANDSLIDE IN SOMEONE ELSE'S LIFE THROUGH OUR ACTIONS.

Taking ownership of my experience in the relationship was the first pivotal step I needed to rebuild the trust. And over twenty years later, I've come to understand that I am my dad. Many of you have been my dad. Sure, you might not have ever said the words he used, but we have created a landslide in someone else's life through our actions. That doesn't make us bad people. It makes us wrong, and we're all going to be wrong from time to time. And when we can own that, we can start to show up differently.

RENEGOTIATE THE RELATIONSHIP

I have a friend who sweeps things under the rug every time something difficult happens. It's easier for him to compartmentalize and move forward than it is to have a difficult conversation and express his needs. You'll hear him occasionally comment on a situation or a person's past behavior. The lack of trust is still there, lurking under the surface of the relationship, though my friend never addresses it outright.

You cannot heal what you do not talk about. Repairing broken trust is possible, but it's uncomfortable and takes time. It requires commitment on both people's part to address the situation(s), the impacts, and what we need from each other moving forward. This is what renegotiating the relationship looks like. The reality is you're never going back to the same

YOU CANNOT HEAL WHAT YOU DO NOT TALK ABOUT.

relationship. You can't. It won't work. Trust can no longer bloom there. There is an undercurrent of insecurity that lingers in that space, so we must find a new space to show up in together. We must commit to showing up in different ways that serve ourselves, each other, and the relationship.

Renegotiating the relationship is about getting clear about what we both need from each other. This process is about being honest in the moment about what you need in the future. It's also accepting that you might change your mind as the relationship unfolds, and you have every right to renegotiate as many times as you need.

Effective management requires a constant checking in and renegotiation of the relationship. It's inquiring how each other is doing in the relationship, what's working and not working, and what needs to happen differently in the weeks to come. When we make these types of conversations casual and safe, we open the door for trust to grow. I had a part-time employee who started another job while also working for me. We both sat down before she began her new role to explore what this meant for our relationship and how things might look different moving forward. She said she would need me to be even more flexible for about a month as she was onboarded in her new role. As a result, we moved our one-on-ones to 6:00 pm. I expressed that I didn't care when the work got done as long as we responded to clients and their experience was not impacted. Each week, we kept each other in the loop with how things were going and if we needed anything different. As a result, we navigated the situation with grace and took our communication to a new level.

It's important to know the difference between renegotiating your needs versus assuming control in a relationship. In his book *The Mastery of Love*, Don Miguel Ruiz said this about people who exhibit control: "I have to control you because I don't respect you. I have to be responsible for you, because whatever happens to you is going to hurt me, and I want to avoid pain." Control sets every relationship up for failure. Controlling behavior appears as ultimatums, tracking or monitoring someone's moves, isolating them from others, using guilt to get a desired outcome, or constantly criticizing everything they do. Control is always rooted in fear. Fear causes us to lash out and punish people for how they hurt us. That's the difference between control and expressing your needs. Expressing your needs in a relationship is never punitive. You're not dictating how people must show up. You're clearly expressing what you need out of love so you can show up as your best self. The other person gets to make a conscious choice whether that's something they feel they can honor. From there, we all get to make informed decisions. If they can't honor your need, you can choose to walk away.

Expressing healthy needs from a place of love in a relationship might sound like the following:
For me to show up as my best in this relationship, I need:

- to know I can communicate with someone who will listen and not belittle me
- to spend quality time just focused on each other
- to have a partner who isn't going to bail when things get tough
- someone who aligns with my values of family and spirituality
- some weekly time apart where I hang out with my friends

These expressions are clear and kind. The other person is free to show up however they please, but they now clearly understand what you believe you need from the relationship at this moment.

Finally, the process of renegotiating the relationship will require patience and often more than one conversation. I'm not even sure it's healthy to unpack everything in one conversation. Both people in the relationship need time to process, reflect, think, and reengage when they have more clarity. Relationships change. People change. And with those changes come a different set of needs and wants. It is then that new agreements must be made. When we fail to renegotiate what we need, we stay stuck to the past and unable to grow together into the future.

ASK FOR/EXTEND FORGIVENESS

A man once came up to me after my keynote program on trust and said, "What hit me is when you said silence is the biggest threat to any organization or relationship." He explained that he and his brother had gotten into a big argument about their aging mother, and they had to figure out a different arrangement for her moving forward. They both wanted what was best for her, but they didn't see eye-to-eye on how to get there. He told me that he sent a text during my program apologizing to his brother and letting him know how much he cared about him. We talked about how the path to rebuilding trust is vulnerable, and forgiveness is key.

Ruth Bell Graham said, "A happy marriage is simply the union of two good forgivers." I'd expand on that and say that every healthy relationship is a partnership of two great forgivers. You cannot be in any long-term relationship without disappointing each other at some point. There will be moments if you're together long enough that you drag your bad day home to the people you love the most. You will unconsciously say something that triggers the other person's insecurities, or you will get frustrated and say something that lacks tact. This moment doesn't represent our best and how we regularly communicate with each other. In those moments, we must care enough about the relationship to accept each other's humanness and extend forgiveness to both ourselves and the other person.

EVERY HEALTHY RELATIONSHIP IS A PARTNERSHIP OF TWO GREAT FORGIVERS.

FORGIVENESS IS ONE OF THE HIGHEST EXPRESSIONS OF LOVE WE DEMONSTRATE.

Forgiveness is a spiritual practice of both awareness and grace. Forgiveness is the awareness that you, or someone else, did not show up at your or their best, and you are extending the grace to move forward without repeated punishment. I think many of us struggle with forgiveness. Sometimes we feel we deserve to sit in pain for what we did. Other times, we say we want to forgive, but we don't know how to get to that place. Love is the only way. That might sound "touchy-feely" to some of you, but I believe it's true. Forgiveness is one of the highest expressions of love we demonstrate.

The best way I've learned to grant forgiveness is by choosing to believe that everyone in life is doing the best they know how based on their current level of awareness. That might be hard for some of you to accept, but I'd encourage you to look back on your life when you made some "not so good" decisions. That wasn't your best self. When you made those decisions, you often responded based on fear, insecurities, and a desire to feel wanted and seen. That doesn't make those choices right, moral, ethical, or relationship-focused. Forgiveness doesn't mean everyone in life just gets a permission slip for their behavior, and you must accept it because they "did the best they knew how to do." No. You, me, and everyone else are responsible for our behavior. We must accept the rewards and consequences that come with our choices. That's part of being an adult and a leader. But forgiveness allows me to learn from it and then let it all go so I don't hold myself or someone else hostage to the past.

Forgiveness has nothing to do with forgetting what happened, approving of the behavior, or repairing the relationship with someone else. Forgiveness is about making peace with the situation so that you can move forward unencumbered. Forgiveness doesn't require clarity, approval, or acceptance from others. At the time my dad died, there were a lot of things that had gone unsaid. I had to accept that I would never get the opportunity to say to him what I wanted to. My forgiveness did not require his presence or acknowledgment. It required me to acknowledge the hurt I had and then choose to believe he did the best he knew how to do. His best wasn't good enough. It wasn't what I needed at the moment. He didn't know, at that moment, another way of showing up. So for that, I forgave him.

Forgiveness isn't about the other person. Forgiveness is about freedom. It's a freedom that we create so that we can show up as our highest, best selves. There have been plenty of difficult situations in life where I wasn't sure I would be able to forgive. I had a boss blindside me and prevent me from moving forward in a company. I had a partner steal my checkbook and forge my signature. I had an accountant who stole my money and ended up in jail. I've had partners cheat on me. Heck, how many of you watched the finale of *Game of Thrones*? Talk about not being sure if I could forgive. In these difficult moments, the walls close in, and we don't see a way out. It can feel that anger and revenge are the best tools we have. Following through on them can feel good in the short term but costs us a little of ourselves each time. Anger is like a web, and everything gets tangled inside of it. Our love gets trapped there. Bottling up our love, closing off, and keeping everyone at arm's length distance only hurts ourselves and our relationships. Forgiveness is the freedom we're looking for. Forgiveness opens a window to a different way that we could not see before.

We've all been hurt. We all have reasons to be bitter and jaded. But we have so many more reasons to love and move forward. Holding onto that pain and anger doesn't serve anyone, especially you. One of the many beautiful things about being alive is that you can heal. Do not buy into the belief that you are forever scarred, broken, or unlovable. Those are just stories we tell ourselves so that we don't have to put ourselves together. I know people are more addicted to telling the story about their pain than healing it. Being a victim is never a choice. Remaining one is.

When rebuilding trust, I ask myself, "Can I stay in this relationship without holding this person to repeated punishment for what transpired?" If the answer is no, then I know the best choice is for me to exit the relationship. It's okay to say no. It takes high self-awareness to acknowledge you're not at a point to continue the relationship without sacrificing yourself in the process. It doesn't have to be forever, but maybe it's for a period of time. I need time to heal. We both deserve the opportunity to learn from our actions and grow. We cannot do that when someone constantly holds us to our past. Sometimes the hurt and pain are too great at the moment to see a way forward. Honor that feeling and know that it's coming from a place of love.

Sometimes the answer to the question, "Can I stay in this relationship without holding this person to repeated punishment for what transpired?" is a clear "Yes." Other times the answer is a cautious, "I don't know." The willingness to try is enough. For many of us, forgiveness is not something we do, and then it's over. Maybe it is for very enlightened people, but sometimes, I can be petty. I clearly haven't achieved enlightenment yet. For me, forgiveness is sometimes a day-by-day process of acknowledging what I'm feeling, reminding myself that people have done the best they knew how, and then re-forgiving as much and as often as necessary. I might show up in the relationship a little skeptical or anxious, but I'm hopeful. I don't keep rehashing the past, and I put more faith in the future and our willingness to grow together.

WHAT DO YOU DO WHEN YOU DON'T KNOW HOW TO FORGIVE?

Sometimes the transgression in your relationship might be so overwhelming that you don't feel you can forgive. Honor that feeling in the present moment.

Sometimes letting go is the most loving thing we can do for ourselves and others. You never have to let go of the love you feel and the beautiful memories you created. Still, you can give yourself permission to let go of the pain, the uncertainty, the confusion, and the lack of clarity that is holding both people back from their full potential. Letting go in the present moment offers us the beautiful opportunity to reconnect in the future as fresh new people, not bits and pieces of who we once were.

YOUR ROAD TO YES!

The most difficult part of a relationship is the ending. When two people are not able to live up to each other's expectations, they are often left disappointed, hurt, and even angry. It is easy just to want to end all contact immediately, but the end of a relationship requires love. That means owning your part in the breakdown, acknowledging both parties did their best in making decisions, and forgiving yourself and the other person. It is in our ability to extend love in the most difficult moments that we can learn, heal, and not repeat the same patterns in our next relationship.

It's easy to leave a relationship angry. Anger prevents us from acknowledging our part in the dysfunction, and it allows us to play the victim when our friends rally around us. However, emotional maturity and growth challenge us to leave relationships from a place of love. Love requires us to acknowledge our sadness for losing something that was once special to us. It is accepting that we're no longer on the same journey or able to give each other what we need. Love is putting yourself in spaces that allow you to honor the best of who you are, and love lets the other person go so they can do the same. Anger is easy. It doesn't require work. Love is hard because it tests your values and your character. But, in the end, it's the only thing that can bring you peace and ensure you don't drag that baggage into the next relationship. Love always wins.

There was a period in my life when I thought I knew the person I would marry. Without any prior conversation or arguments, the relationship came crashing down. To say I was devastated would be an understatement. It took some time, but I learned to find forgiveness because I realized that person was struggling. He didn't know how to express his emotions and needs, nor did he understand how to allow me to be a part of his journey. I also had to forgive myself. I teach communication. I blamed myself for not being intuitive enough to know something was going on. I got consumed in the "What if" game. What if I had done this. What if that hadn't happened. None of that mattered. The past was the past, and torturing myself with what-ifs served no one. I had to let all that go and remind myself that it's not my responsibility to own someone else's feelings. I acknowledged that I did the best I knew how to do in that relationship at the time. I eventually found myself on a hike at

Sabino Canyon in Tucson, Arizona. It was there that I sat down by a creek, listened to the water, and wrote this poem:

> *I release my love for you to the universe.*
> *I offer it to the person who can love you*
> *The way you need to be loved,*
> *Who can protect your heart,*
> *And who can help you grow.*
> *I hold onto your beautiful memory*
> *While releasing this energy from my soul.*
> *May the universe conspire to bring you*
> *Exactly what and who you need.*
> *I love you, and I release you...*
> *I love you, and I release you...*
> *I love you, and I release you...*

I said this poem aloud until I believed what I was saying. I walked out of the canyon with no desire to return to the relationship. I had love in my heart, and I was ready to move forward.

DEMONSTRATE A CHANGE IN BEHAVIOR

Apologizing is important when you mess up, but that apology is only sincere when backed up by a change in behavior. Manipulation happens when we say all the right things in a relationship but then demonstrate the same behaviors that erode trust.

When we listen to each other, understand each other's needs, and change our behavior, we demonstrate intentional effort. It's an effort that people appreciate and can stand beside. Remember: every action you take in a relationship must work to build incremental trust. When rebuilding trust, those incremental trust deposits are critical. People don't want to see you "trying" to do it. They want to see you doing it.

It can feel overwhelming when you want to save a relationship, but you're unsure how to make it happen. You might be tempted to dive all in and change a bunch of what you see as your "negative behaviors." Working on yourself is important. Getting addicted to it and feeling like you need to change everything about yourself is not. It's always good to take a step back and focus on changing just a couple of meaningful behaviors in the beginning. The goal is to make quick changes but also to follow through and make them stick! That's always the hard part. Once you weave those behaviors into your regular habits, you can decide if making more changes is necessary.

Choose one or two key behaviors that, if demonstrated, would have a significant impact on your ability to repair trust in your relationship. Maybe for some of you, it's communicating your thoughts and feelings more transparently. Other people might say they need to take the initiative at work and not wait to be told what to do. I've coached individuals who said the action that would have the most significant impact would be going to therapy, or creating a "no-fly zone" at night where they stop working and spend time with their family, or stop trying to fix people and start showing empathy. Trust that you either know the answer or that you can have a conversation with the individual and decide, based upon that conversation, an appropriate course of action.

CHOOSE ONE OR TWO KEY BEHAVIORS THAT, IF DEMONSTRATED, WOULD HAVE A SIGNIFICANT IMPACT ON YOUR ABILITY TO REPAIR TRUST IN YOUR RELATIONSHIP.

A few questions you might ask yourself when trying to decide on what a change of behavior might look like in the relationship include:

- What barriers are preventing me from showing up the way I want?
- What steps can I take now to remove some of those barriers?
- What is the most important change I can make right now to rebuild trust?
- How am I improving this person's life?
- What does this other person need/want from me?
- What value am I bringing to this relationship?

Have you ever found yourself in a relationship where you've taken ownership, asked for forgiveness, renegotiated what each other needed, and demonstrated a behavior change, but the other person expects you to constantly "win" their trust back? My experience is that you can't win that game, and the best option is to leave. I coached a client who was put on a performance improvement plan and then given coaching so she could do the work to rebuild trust and credibility. At the end of our coaching, she accomplished all the success metrics outlined by her and management. We conducted a 360 review, and all the feedback from peers and direct reports was positive. The outlier was her boss. She had a more negative view of this individual, and no matter how hard the client worked, it was never enough. It was clear that the client was never going to "win" her manager's trust back, and they only gave her a coach so they could justify her exit from the organization. This individual's boss had no desire to make the relationship a partnership. It had become a game of chess, and manipulation was her strategy for getting what she wanted. Nothing my client did would be good enough. Her boss chose to see her through the lens of her past. It wasn't fair to my client. It wasn't fair to the organization. And frankly, it wasn't fair to their relationship. The people worth your time and energy will not see your relationship as a game to win. They'll see it as a place where we learn, grow, and move forward together.

I stated earlier in the book that trust is your biggest competitive advantage, and silence is your biggest threat. You can't stay silent if you want to rebuild trust with someone else. Both people need the opportunity to be heard, share their feelings, and express what they need moving forward. You'll need to check in occasionally with each other, address any concerns, and recommit.

REBUILDING TRUST IS A TRIAL OF PATIENCE.

Rebuilding trust is a trial of patience. The process will often take longer than you think or expect. Be patient. Give yourself and the relationship time to navigate through all these steps. Remember: these steps are not linear. Sometimes the forgiveness won't come until you have consistently demonstrated the change in behavior for a while. Other times, you will have to forgive yourself before you dare to take ownership of something you did. There is no one right way to navigate through the process of rebuilding trust. It's situational. I hope knowing the process is fluid gives you some comfort that there's not just one right way. Make yourself available to the other person and commit to talking as much as they need. Make sure in the process of communicating that you demonstrate transparency, tact, and togetherness.

I can't promise that this process will save every relationship you want, but I can promise it will give you a better chance. Second chances are a gift. I'm not sure if magic really exists in life, but second chances fill us with hope, and that has to be one of the most magical things we can feel. Hope catapults us into a new way of thinking and acting. It is the spark to a new beginning. And you, yes, you, are always worthy of a new beginning.

CHAPTER SEVEN
SUMMARY

- Beginnings are easy. Staying together is the difficult part.
- Ask yourself, "Is this a pattern, or just a moment?"
- We find a way through, or we find a way out, but we're not remaining stuck!
- Four steps to repairing trust:
  1. Take ownership
  2. Renegotiate the relationship
  3. Ask for/Extend forgiveness
  4. Demonstrate a change in behavior
- The four steps to repairing trust are *NOT* a linear process.
- Ownership is about accepting full responsibility for your experience in the relationship.
- You cannot heal what you do not talk about.
- Renegotiating the relationship is about getting clear about what we both need from each other moving forward if the relationship is going to be successful.
- The path to rebuilding trust is vulnerable, and forgiveness is key.
- Every healthy relationship is a partnership of two great forgivers.
- Forgiveness is one of the highest expressions of love we demonstrate.
- Rebuilding trust is a trial of patience.

CHAPTER EIGHT

NOW IT'S UP TO YOU

*You were born a light
In a world that can feel dark.
Never stop burning!*

I stated in the beginning that the goal for all of us is to be in relationships built on yes. Hear me when I tell you: You. Deserve. That. You owe it to yourself to be in relationships where transparency, tact, and togetherness are consistently present. That should be the standard, not the exception. That doesn't mean you won't have problems or that it won't be uncomfortable at times. It means that you're committed to figuring it out together. It means you will always have each other's back in the process.

You purchased and read this book for what it could do for you and your relationships. I hope you found the messages you didn't even know you needed. You've reflected on yourself, learned new strategies, and visualized what a relationship with stronger trust looks like. Now it's up to you to apply what you've learned.

Choose a relationship in your life that you would like to build more trust in over the next several weeks. That relationship could be with yourself or with another person. Next, identify why the trust might not be where you want it. Maybe you've just gotten so busy that you haven't been checking in as regularly as you should. Perhaps you haven't been as transparent as you should with the other person about something, or maybe you realize that you tend to jump in with solutions when what that person needs from you is to empathize first. Once you know how you might be contributing to the lack of trust, now it's your time to take decisive action. Identify specific actions from the book that you could take to start building back trust incrementally. If you're unsure what actions to take, then muster the courage to ask, "What can I do to be a better partner/friend/colleague for you?" Remember: It's not about the relationship changing overnight; it's about your ability to show intentional effort.

YOUR GUIDING QUESTION ON TRUST

I know all the strategies and concepts we discussed can be daunting initially, and you might question where to start. Therefore, I want to challenge you to create a guiding question. You can ask yourself this question when you need a reminder about how to move forward with trust. A guiding question helps simplify the process when things get busy, when people are having an off day, and when you're making strategic decisions about the future.

WHAT CHOICE WOULD I MAKE RIGHT NOW IF I WAS FOCUSED ON BUILDING TRUST?

The guiding question that has served me well over the past several months is, "What choice would I make right now if I was focused on building trust?" The answers have been insightful. Sometimes I decided to say something because I knew I wouldn't be able to move forward unless I did. Sometimes I acknowledged I just needed to keep my mouth shut. It was my issue, and I needed to keep it on my side of the street and deal with it. We can't bring up everything that annoys or bothers us in a relationship. That would be exhausting. Sometimes I realize I haven't been investing in the relationship like I should, and I need to do better. It's been a provocative question for me. I encourage you to develop your own guiding question that will serve you and your relationships well moving forward. Feel free to use one of the following examples or create your own.

1. How would I communicate if I were both truthful and kind?
2. What would I say if I loved this person enough to tell the truth?
3. How would I respond if I was focused on being a team player?
4. What choice is in the best interest of the relationship?
5. What would my "best self" do?
6. How would I want someone to treat my mom?

I ended chapter one by saying, "Your choices should always lead to yes." Answering your guiding question will help ensure you're doing your part to make yes a cornerstone of your relationships.

A WORKPLACE OF TRUST AND BELONGING IS EVERYONE'S RESPONSIBILITY

The other benefit of your guiding question is that it will help you do your part in building a stronger culture of trust and belonging. Building a culture of trust and belonging is everyone's responsibility in the workplace.

Executives have a role in setting the vision for the culture, providing the expectations and resources to bring that culture to life, and ensuring they role-model the values they say are important. It is a vital, necessary role. A few questions I believe all executive leadership teams need to discuss include:

BUILDING A CULTURE OF TRUST AND BELONGING IS EVERYONE'S RESPONSIBILITY IN THE WORKPLACE.

1. What is the vision for the organizational culture?
2. How are we communicating and promoting people that live out the culture?
3. How is our culture adding strategic value to the organization?
4. What resources do our managers need to bring the culture to life?
5. How are we directly or indirectly rewarding bad behavior across the business?
6. What pockets of the company are not living our values? Why?

Managers impact the workplace culture probably more than anyone else in the organization because they have the biggest influence over what behaviors are rewarded, coached, and promoted. How managers communicate influences the culture and whether it's a place employees want to stay or leave. If you want a strong and thriving workplace culture, you have to invest in your awareness and communication skills. Spaces of trust and belonging depend on it. The more emotionally intelligent (EQ) our managers become, the more they raise the EQ of the whole organization.

THE MORE EMOTIONALLY INTELLIGENT (EQ) OUR MANAGERS BECOME, THE MORE THEY RAISE THE EQ OF THE WHOLE ORGANIZATION.

Individual contributors are the service heroes of every organization because they generally have more direct contact with customers than anyone else. How they show up will ultimately determine the guest experience. We owe it to these heroes to help them understand who they are at their best and how to recharge emotionally when they feel drained. We must provide them with feedback and coaching on the impact of their presence.

Below are five questions on trust that every manager can ask their team members during one-on-ones to develop deeper awareness, drive accountability, and reinforce the culture of trust they say they want:

1. What did you do this week to build trust in the team or with customers?
2. What, if anything, was bothering you that you addressed directly?
3. What actions did you take to make others feel safe?
4. What actions did you take to make others feel seen and valued?
5. What can you do to help build more trust among the team?

These five questions allow the space for people to reflect. They enable managers to recognize and reinforce desired behaviors, giving them an introduction to coaching around trust.

I BELIEVE IN YOU

This book has prepared you with the mindset and strategies you need to build and keep the trust of the personal and professional relationships you value. Trust-based leadership is not a new concept. It's just one that never gets old. It is the type of leadership that brings out the best in oneself and others.

It takes incredible amounts of courage to be someone who builds trust. Trust is not mutually exclusive from strength, care, and inclusivity. Trust is the intersection of all these attributes. They are tightly woven together, and they cannot be separated if we are to create any type of relationship where people feel they can show up, be authentic, and become better versions of themselves.

Someone out there is waiting for you right now. They need your presence to reimagine how they see themselves and show up in the world. Love them enough to tell them the truth. Make it safe for them to open up and do whatever you can to help make them feel a little less alone. Prove to them that relationships built on yes change everything. If no one tells you they believe in you, I believe in you.

Go out and make your mark in the world, and always do it through trust.

INFINITE

From the moment you were born
You became a bright light
In what can sometimes feel
Like a dark and unrelenting world.

Your presence gave people hope
they could be better,
dream bigger,
love deeper.
And you did all of that
Just by being yourself.

You walked by strangers
Who felt they had to
Stay silent and stay hidden —
just to stay alive.
You stood beside them
Like a tidal wave of safety
And your presence made them feel
They can step out and be seen,
Speak up and be safe,
And step back into the glorious light
They were born with.

You taught people to
Forgive themselves for ever believing
They had to hustle
To be loved,
To be seen,
To feel worthy,
To be accepted.

YOUR ROAD TO YES!

If there was ever a moment,
A minute, a second,
In someone's life
Where they believed in themselves,
It was in your presence.
And for that
You have changed everything.

One day,
When your spark fades into the night,
You will glance back
And see the whole world on fire.
Lit up by the difference you made.
And you can rest knowing
You made the world
A kinder, gentler, and more trusting place.
And for that, you cannot die.
Your presence is and forever will be
Infinite.

ACKNOWLEDGMENTS

Susan Patton
You're the best sister a brother could have. Thank you for always being my biggest supporter and making me laugh. I'm grateful we get to do life together.

Jenna Reese
Thank you for your constant friendship and for always picking up the phone. You're my safe space to brainstorm ideas and ask challenging questions. You make me better.

Joel Sarmiento
Thank you for being a guiding force in my life in the past couple years and teaching me about trust, love, and having each other's back.

Captain Dave Tuck
Your leadership ignited a spark in me, and your presence has changed people's lives. I hope you never forget the difference you make.

Monica Rothgery
You believed in me, gave me a chance, and ultimately changed the course of my life. You are this journey, this book, and in everything I do. Thank you.

Greg Creed
You are my north star in leadership. Thank you for being a role model to so many. You teach us that being our full authentic selves is enough, is needed, and is what changes company culture for the better.

Abby Ross Hopper
Thank you for demonstrating the power of transparency and how great leaders love people enough to tell them the truth.

National Speakers Association Mastermind
Special thanks to Ted Ma, Lisa Ryan, Debbie Peterson, and John Register for loving, challenging, and pushing me every step of the way for the past few years. You've made me a better speaker and author. I love y'all.

YOUR ROAD TO YES!

NCAA Division II Staff
Thank you for your partnership over the years and trusting my message with your student athletes and coaches across the United States. You've opened so many doors for me, and I hope that together we've been able to do the same for others.

US Chamber of Commerce Staff
Thank you, Raymond Towle and Karyn MacRae, for allowing me to teach at the Institute for Organization Management (IOM). You've both been mentors and advocates. I'm better because of your feedback, generosity, and friendship.

Dave Hare
You went from being the first business leader to ever hire me to someone who is a friend. Thank you for so many years of friendship, opportunity, and encouragement. You make the spaces you're in and the people you're around better.

Chad Bock and Aaron Kessinger
Thank you for trusting me over the years, never giving up on me, and showing me unconditional love.

Kam Bains (Singh Styles)
You're the most stylish man I know! Thank you for customizing my suits, making me look better than I know how to do on my own, and for your friendship over the years. Keep making the world a more beautiful place.

Jeremy Ryan
You're such a gifted photographer, artist, and video producer. I'm thankful our worlds crashed into one another. Thank you for taking the photos for my website and this book. You know how to bring out the best in others.

Shaina Nielson
I lucked out finding such a talented graphic designer. Thank you for being on this journey with me over the years and bringing all my content to life. Your work is art, and it allows people to see themselves in it. That's a gift!

ABOUT THE AUTHOR

Justin Patton is an international speaker, award-winning author, and executive coach. His mission is to empower leaders to lead, love, and communicate better in their lives. Justin believes trust is our biggest competitive advantage, and he challenges leaders to rethink how they show up and use their presence.

Justin earned a master's degree in education from The University of Louisville, taught high school English and creative writing for five years, and then went on to teach leaders at Anthem and Yum! Brands before starting his speaking and coaching company. Justin is a faculty member of the Institute for Organization Management, and he has expertise in body language, executive presence, and emotional intelligence. Additionally, Justin is a member of the International Coach Federation and National Speakers Association.

Justin's high-energy style, relatable storytelling, and relevant messages make him a sought-after keynote speaker.

For more information about Justin and his work, visit **justinpatton.com**. You can also follow him across all social media for a dose of inspiration and leadership tips.